AT HOME WITH CHEF MARK PHILLIPS

CONTENTS

v	PREFACE
viii	FOREWORD
x	INTRODUCTION
13	WHERE DO I START?
35	SOUP, SALADS, & SANDWICHES
69	APPETIZERS & SNACKS
105	COMING FROM WHERE I'M FROM
141	WHAT'S FOR DINNER?
177	EAT YOUR VEGETABLES
211	THE SWEET SPOT
245	IT'S 5 O'CLOCK SOMEWHERE
288	ACKNOWLEDGMENTS

PREFACE

WITH LOVE,
Chef Mark Phillips

I always knew I was meant to write a cookbook. Over the years, I wrote down a few recipes here and there. When COVID-19 shut down my business and the world, I suddenly had a lot of unwanted free time. My work as a professional chef is centered around my clients—creating meals in their homes, cooking for customers in restaurants, and catering events. All of that came to a halt. I found myself evaluating life, my career, and like many of you; cooking more at home.

I cooked at home before COVID, but the pandemic gave me more time with family. I was living with my bonus sister Erica, her husband Karey, and my niece Kenzie. They became the focus of my mealtime creations. I had to be incredibly thoughtful about my process since Kenzie was my little kitchen helper.

Cooking for people is my passion. It was so challenging to lose the thing I love to do the most. I am sure many of you can relate, as many people had their lives upended during the pandemic.

Social media helped me stay connected to my clients and customers, and it played a significant role in compiling the recipes in this book. I would post pictures of my culinary creations, and my followers would ask me, "How did you cook that?" or "Can you send me the recipe?" When my friends and family members started calling and texting me, asking me the same thing, I knew I wanted to use my extra hours to write a cookbook.

Creativity in the kitchen comes naturally to me, but I had to face my fears about sharing my passion for cooking in writing. I remember watching "Fear Not" by Iyanla Vanzant on the OWN network during my writing process. That series motivated me to bring this book to life. It inspired me to overcome my disappointment of being unable to share my Love of food by cooking for customers and clients; instead, it propelled me to share my recipes for everyone to enjoy.

I am fortunate I was able to channel my passion for food into something good during a time when things were bad. I knew at some point we would celebrate and entertain again. I want you to use my book to cook something new and to get to know a little bit about me.

Food brings people together. I want to share my Love for cooking with you and your family. I hope you enjoy stepping into my world and taking this journey with me. These recipes are meant to be experienced in the years to come. They are selected for you from a place of Love and Light!

FOREWORD

"I feel like cooking" It was those four words that lead me to experience a taste of Chef Mark and be a part of the birthing of Southern Temptation. The key word here is, "feel". When Chef Mark prepares a Meal for you, you can taste the feeling of love and passion from his creation. Through my daughter Genia's introduction, we came instant friends, extended family and a heart and soul tie.

It all began when Mark, my newfound bonus son, expressed his desire to me to cook up some deliciousness, as we strolled through Piedmont Park one Sunday afternoon. He had recently graduated from culinary school and we both were new to Atlanta and shared a love for art and photography. This was a designated art inspiration day with our cameras in tow. For Mark the creativity extended beyond the camera lens to the kitchen to express his culinary artistry.

My question to Mark's statement, "I feel like cooking" was "well, what do you feel like cooking?" His response and that first meal led to a journey of Sunday meals that to this day has become a tradition of love and connection around mouthwatering, belly filling, soul satisfying, scrumdelalicious food. Shared with a crew of newfound friends and family that we adorn as our ever expanding "Love Circle". The first meal that Mark described, for which I more than willingly offered my kitchen for preparation was a menu that at this moment leaves me craving for more. Salmon Florentine, collard greens, baked macaroni & cheese with a tossed green salad.

There are many recipes in this book I've had the pleasure, honor, and experience to partake of. Some of my favorite along with the previously mention dishes are, Baked Sweet Potato with Broccoli Pesto, Kale, Quinoa & Apple Salad, Thai Coconut Curry Vegetables & Noodles, Crab Stuffed Mushrooms, and my favorite birthday treat, Cheesecake Balls, YES!!!

I've been a fan flowing foodie since day one. From our Sunday dinners to countless meals prepared for my company MaD Miracles monthly Miracle Minded Brunch and special events to personal meal preparation. All created by this once eager culinary graduate to now master chef. There are also new recipes I am excited to step into my favorite roles as taste tester to experience for the first time. What I am certain of is a Chef Mark creation is a foodgasm for my soul.

May every dish you prepare from these pages bring a spark of joy to your table, yumminess to your mouth, comfort to your belly, and satisfaction to your soul knowing it was created with the utmost love for you and your nourishment. Whenever the opportunity presents itself to taste any of these delectable dishes personally prepared go with an empty stomach and an open heart and let yourself be filled by Chef Mark Phillips your culinary artist.

Joyfully – Jaaz Jones

First Client and Bonus Mom!

INTRODUCTION

One thing people consistently ask me is, "How do I cook this?" or "What can I do with that?" I will be honest; I often cook without writing down my recipes. I would not say that "winging it" is a chef-only trait; think about your grandmother's special dish or your uncle's signature BBQ sauce and how they can recreate it the same way each time without referring to a recipe. Over these past few years, I have been making an effort to write recipes for a book. It has taken me about two years to compile these recipes and half of that year formatting them so you can recreate the dishes.

Cooking: the art or practice of preparing food; cookery! One of the many definitions you will find when you browse the definition of "Cooking".

When someone asks me how to cook something or to send them a recipe, my first thought is, "it's easy," do a little bit of this, add some of that, and finish with some of the other. If I say that out loud, people often give me a faraway stare. I guess it is like an accountant telling me how to do payroll or taxes, I would look at them like a deer caught in the headlights.

Although I am a professional chef, I wanted to create a cookbook to inspire individuals to jazz up dinner ideas, introduce new tasty treats for entertaining, explore dishes so delicious they might consider adopting a diet of mostly vegetables, and craft a cocktail while planning something sweet for dessert. I believe food brings people together, and in a time where everyone is attached to their electronic devices, I hope to inspire you to create something delicious and encourage you to fellowship with the ones you love.

The kitchen is a place I know well. It is my favorite room in the house—the heart of any home. My Love for cooking started when I was young. I grew up in Winston-Salem, North Carolina, where I got my first introduction to food—southern food, to be exact. As early as I can remember, preparing and sharing food was intricately tied to the Love of family or the gathering of people you care for over food. My childhood home was the place to be for holidays, backyard barbecues, or just because. Nine times out of ten, my home life centered around food.

Most kids my age were into video games, sports, or music, but my passions were (and still are) art and cooking.

We didn't have access to the variety of foods I have grown to love as an adult, but my mother surely made the best out of what we had. My Uncle Joe had a small farm with all sorts of goodies in his backyard. There were chickens and dogs running around and a garden with collards, green beans, tomatoes, and more. On visits to his home, we would go into the hen house to see if the chickens had laid eggs. His farm was my first experience with "farm-to-table." My mother and aunts were constantly gathering in the kitchen, preparing food for the family, and some of us kids were right there watching and learning.

I remember early on in middle school, one of my teachers asked what we wanted to be when we grew up. My first response was "artist" or "businessman." Art is my first Love, and I still paint to this day. However, I was not eager to become a "starving artist" because I had experienced hardship in my childhood. I associated being a businessman with wearing suits and having success and wealth.

In school, we had a class called "Home-Ec or Home Economics," where my structural culinary experiences began. One food that stood out was monkey bread which we made with canned biscuits dressed with cinnamon sugar and butter. Thanks to my experience cooking at home, I found I could experiment with the basic recipe and create something new. I blended my artistic side with my Love of food.

Fast-forward to high school. I took a vocational class at the career center along with core classes. Ms. Darlene Clinkscales introduced me to cooking on an institutional level. With her guidance, I applied to and graduated from Johnson & Wales University, a school famous for its culinary and hospitality curriculum. College gave me more than a degree. I acquired technical skills and had leadership and management training. I learned the standards and practices of logistics, operations, and marketing for the culinary and hospitality industries.

I attended the Johnson and Wales campus in Miami, Florida. My time in Miami had a significant impact on the way I cook. South Florida is a vacation destination for the entire world. You can get food from nearly every region on the globe. Miami is famous for its diverse neighborhoods, and I was exposed to many Caribbean, Latin, and South American cultures. I started to build my cooking style, which I call "American Fusion."

After graduation, I spent my first years working my way up the culinary ranks: intern, prep-cook, line cook, head cook, and executive chef. I now own **Southern Temptation**, a catering, personal chef, and consulting brand, which has afforded me access to a wide range of clients. Cooking is my passion, and I am blessed to do what I love for a living.

Now that you have a little background on who I am and how and why I wrote this book, I will give you a tour of the chapters and explain why I selected these categories.

Where Do I Start? is a reintroduction to your kitchen. Think of it as a "back to the basics" chapter to provide you with terminology, measurements, equipment, and the means and knowledge to read the recipes and understand what items you need to create your dish.

Next are the three Ss—**Soups, Salads, and Sandwiches**. Whether you're looking for lunch recipes, side dishes, or hearty main meals, you'll love the options in this chapter. The simple combination of soup and a sandwich brings me pure joy. Salads can be fun and festive because there is no limit to what you can add to create layers of tasty goodness.

I believe I get the most enjoyment in creating **Appetizers & Snacks**. Everyone finds something irresistible in the perfect, bite-sized treats. They are tantalizing to the tastebuds and keep guests coming back for more. The **Appetizers & Snacks** section is designed to help you create memorable food for your guests regardless of how large or small the occasion is.

I dedicated a chapter to the southern culture I grew up cooking and eating. Here you will find classic staples along with my south Florida influences. Each recipe pays homage to my family and extended family. The chapter is named after a song from one of my favorite male vocalists, Anthony Hamilton, who also happens to be from North Carolina. The lead single from his debut album entitled "**Comin' From Where I From**."

Most of us have heard or used the phrase "**What's For Dinner**." I compiled recipes I love to cook and dinners I hope will inspire you—whether you follow my recipe "to the T" (which I hope you do) or add your own twist.

The chapter **Eat Your Vegetables** takes you on a flavorful journey centered around vegetables. It sheds a tasty new light on what many consider side dishes. I bring veggies to the forefront. Vegetables can be the star of the show, and I feature them in some fun and tasty recipes.

The Sweet Spot is dedicated to desserts. These dessert recipes are creamy, flakey, fruity, and everything in between. Baking is a beautiful science; you cannot take liberties with the measurements. I give you tips and tricks to improve your results.

Whether it's shaken or stirred, who doesn't love a good cocktail? The final chapter is called **It's 5'o'clock Somewhere**. I open by providing you with a bit of wine education and background on spirits. You can use this knowledge to create my drink selections or your own.

Thank you for choosing my cookbook! It is exciting to share my passion for food with you, your friends, and your family. Now, let's get cooking!

NEXT

WHERE DO I START?

Kitchen Reintroduction

KITCHEN REINTRODUCTION

Most of us grew up in homes where our parents collected basic kitchen utensils and equipment over the years. Some cherished items may have been in your family for generations. As a chef, I have more utensils than the average home cook. The popularity of cooking shows, social media chefs, online shopping, and infomercials have introduced all kinds of new kitchen gadgetry to the home cook. Determining which items are beneficial could be challenging or overwhelming without guidance. I put together a list of the most functional items to make your cooking experience more manageable.

My motto is "Work smarter, not harder," I hope this chapter will help you choose quality over quantity. Whether you have a large chef's kitchen or a studio with minimal space, it is essential to stock a fully functional and multi-purpose minimalist kitchen. I will reference the utensils and equipment listed in this chapter throughout my cookbook. I am also sharing terminology to bring you a little bit more into my culinary world.

I want to supply you with some basic terms we use in the industry. You may already know some of these terms, some may be new, and others you may have heard but were unsure of their meaning. The list is compiled from A-to-Z and features vocabulary found in my recipes plus terms which are suitable for general knowledge.

If you're an amateur cook, an accomplished home chef, or even a professional chef, you can appreciate the value of a high-quality knife. A good, sharp, stainless steel knife can make cooking a joy. On the other hand, using a dull, low-grade knife makes cooking a chore; the difference is night and day. I am not a fan of the "cheap knife set," where every blade has a serrated edge; it's the worst (Sorry if that is the set you have. However, I will help you with a bit of knife education). A good kitchen setup doesn't require a thousand knives, each with a specific purpose. A home chef only needs a few knives in their cutlery set to get any job done—provided the blades are made from high-quality, often high-carbon, steel and treated right. A three-piece cutlery set is a good start; a five-piece set should give you all you need.

A basic kitchen conversion chart is your friend. Volume and weight conversions are important resources to have in the kitchen. When halving or doubling a recipe, choosing the correct conversions can make or break your results. This is particularly important in baking, as baking is a science. In The Sweet Spot chapter, I will go into more detail about baking dos and don'ts.

The U.S. system of measurements is based on the old British Imperial system, and the U.S. remains one of the few countries worldwide that hasn't switched to metric measurements. The sheer number of chefs and recipes coming out of the U.S. means understanding this system and how to scale recipes remains a necessity. I have been cooking professionally for years, and sometimes I refer to the charts for a refresher.

Growing up, my mother primarily had non-stick pots and pans and a few stainless steel pans. Non-stick can make the clean-up more effortless, but I prefer stainless steel. A stainless steel skillet will likely be the workhorse of your kitchen. This cookware is used for frying, searing, sautéing, and browning, among other functions. For this reason, it's crucial to pick a high-quality stainless steel skillet that you can use for a lifetime.

Last but not least, is a tip about the internal temperatures of meats. It is imperative to cook your meats to the proper temperature because you do not want anyone to get sick. Beef and game meats are most often cooked to the diner's preference; more recently, pork and fish are prepared to specific internal temperatures. I could go into detail, but you will be fine if you know the basic safe temperature zones.

Now that I have given you a brief overview let's dive in. As you make these recipes, you will notice that I refer to the content in this chapter. Feel free to return to this part of the book for definitions and guides to following my recipes.

KITCHEN ESSENTIALS

LADLE

A ladle is a spoon used for soup, stew, or other foods. Ladles with a bent handle at the top allow you to hook the ladle on the side of a pot and prevent it from falling in.

TONGS

Tongs are a tool used to grip and lift objects instead of holding them directly with your hands. Use tongs for turning meats and tossing vegetables in a skillet. Tongs are made in various sizes and styles—some have rubber handles to protect from heat, and others are made entirely of plastic for ready-to-eat items.

METAL & RUBBER SPATULA

An offset thin blade allows you to get under delicate items like cookies and pancakes. A medium-length edge prevents flipping or picking up foods at an awkward angle. A rubber spatula should be sturdy enough to maneuver heavy dough but flexible enough to get into jar corners. Silicone models are heat-resistant and can be used in pots.

SLOTTED SPOON

Pick a sturdy spoon with a stainless steel handle that will not get too hot. The purpose of the slots or holes is to drain liquid which helps make cooking easier and safer. Use your slotted spoon when removing something from a pan while leaving the yummy juices behind.

WHISK

A whisk is one of the most valuable items in your kitchen. Buy one with thin wires (not thick, heavy ones) to ensure it is well-balanced when whipping egg whites or cream. It is essential to have one with a solid rather than a wire handle to prevent food from getting stuck inside.

GARLIC PRESS

This utensil is a nice shortcut. You won't need to peel or chop. A press works on unpeeled cloves and is dishwasher-safe.

GRATER

A box grater is the most versatile type of grater with six different options to shred, shave, dust, and zest. Instead of purchasing different types of graters, a zester, and a chiffonade, why not choose one tool that can do it all? Choose one with a sturdy handle.

KITCHEN SHEARS

Use your sharpest kitchen shears to cut up a whole chicken and other meats, trim vegetables, strip herbs, and even cut the stems off flowers. Be sure to invest in a sturdy pair with tapered, fine tips and roomy handles.

CITRUS JUICER

Sometimes it's the seemingly insignificant tasks in the kitchen that are more hassle than they're worth. Juicing a lemon or lime is one of those tasks. I grab a fork and go at it; however, a juicer is a better option. The best models are big enough for limes and lemons and have ridges to grip fruit better.

POTATO MASHER

Although a potato masher is a great tool, it usually has an inconvenient and bulky shape that makes closing your drawer challenging. Choose one with a curved head so you can get into the corners of bowls and pots.

VEGETABLE PEELER

A vegetable peeler can speed up your preparation time, whether you're using it to peel potatoes, carrots, or other vegetables. A Y-shaped peeler will give you a better grip than a traditional swivel model for hard-to-peel foods like mangoes and butternut squash.

CAN OPENER

This kitchen utensil is sure to be in every home. Whether you want an electric or a manual opener, choose a safe-cut, or smooth-edge, model which cuts around the outside of the can, rather than the lid. The safe-cut opener produces smooth edges and never lowers the lid into your food.

CORKSCREW

This is essential if you enjoy wine or beer as much as I do. No, it's a necessity in my kitchen. A standard waiter's corkscrew will open beer and wine and take up much less space than a two-armed model.

INSTANT-READ THERMOMETER

A thermometer is vital for reading the accurate temperature of food to ensure it is cooked properly and to help prevent food poisoning. Find a thermometer that is easy to read and shatterproof.

MEASURING CUPS

Measuring cups are used for precisely measuring the volume of liquid or solid cooking ingredients. You'll want measuring cups for both dry and wet ingredients. For dry ingredients, cups are usually sold as a set in the following sizes: 1-cup, ½-cup, 1/3 cup, and ¼ cup. For wet ingredients, you'll need at least a 1-cup measure, but having a more considerable 4-cup measure can save time.

MEASURING SPOONS

Measuring spoons are used to precisely portion smaller amounts of liquid or solid cooking ingredients. Oval-shaped spoons are more likely to fit into spice jars.

PEPPERMILL

Fresh cracked pepper makes a huge difference. Owning a peppermill is a necessity for me. Find a mill with an easily adjustable grind setting that will let you go from coarse to fine. Select a mill with a large hole to make refilling the peppercorns easier.

SALAD SPINNER

A salad spinner is your best friend for achieving a crisp salad. To prevent your greens from going soggy, you'll need to dry them, and "spinning" them is the easiest way to do it. Look for models with a solid bowl for both swishing greens clean and serving them.

TIMER

A timer is as indispensable to cooking as knives and measuring spoons. I use mine for the perfect hardboiled egg (13 minutes). The timer is a must to track exact baking times for cakes. Some digital models allow for multiple alarm settings to follow a roast in the oven, potatoes on the stovetop, and dough in the refrigerator simultaneously.

WIRE MESH COLANDERS

When draining pasta or washing vegetables and salad greens, a colander is essential for your minimalist kitchen. Buy one with a foot at the bottom to ensure your pasta won't sit in the residual puddle in the sink. You can use a small one as a flour sifter in a pinch. A.K.A. "Strainer"

ROLLING PIN

A rolling pin is a cylindrical food preparation utensil used to shape and flatten dough. The two styles of pins are rollers and rods. Roller types consist of a thick cylinder with small handles at each end; rod-type rolling pins are usually thin tapered batons.

MIXING BOWLS

A set of high-quality mixing bowls is a must for mixing salad dressings, spice rubs, marinades, sauces, and even storing leftovers. I prefer stackable glass and/or metal to make storage easier.

KNIVES

CHEF'S KNIFE

The incredibly versatile chef's knife has an 8-to-9-inch blade with a thick handle. It can chop, dice, slice, mince, shred and do just about any other job needed in the kitchen. Invest in a good quality knife that should feel comfortable in your hand; the metal extends from the handle to the edge of the blade and acts as a finger guard while you're chopping.

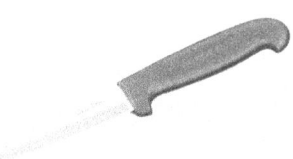

PARING KNIFE

A paring knife is a kitchen knife with a short blade that can be used for a multitude of tasks. You can peel and chop with it, and the small tip is great for fine work like coring strawberries.

BREAD KNIFE

Bread knives have serrated blades that can cut soft bread without crushing it.

SANTOKU KNIFE

The Santoku knife is a Japanese version of the Western-style chef's knife. It's slightly shorter and thinner. It is used in place of the chef's knife by some cooks, especially those who prefer a smaller, lighter blade. Santoku means "three virtues," slicing, dicing, and mincing. This knife is an all-rounder and can do the same jobs as a typical chef's knife.

UTILITY KNIFE

Measuring between 4 and 7 inches in length, the utility knife is usually used for cutting food that is too small for a chef's knife. It's not great for chopping or slicing large items, but the narrow blade and small tip allow it to handle tasks such as thinner slicing, trimming, and filleting even better than a chef's knife.

BONING KNIFE

The boning knife, as its name suggests, is used for separating meat from the bone, filleting fish, and cutting up meat. Smaller boning knives can also be used in place of a paring knife for peeling and trimming veggies. Boning knives are typically about 3 to 8 inches in length with slightly varying blade widths. The blades can be flexible, semi-flexible, or stiff. Stiff blades are the most popular among home cooks due to the enhanced precision of the cut.

CLEAVER KNIFE

The cleaver is usually the bulkiest and heaviest knife in the kitchen. A typical cleaver has a full tang, a thick spine, and a wide blade with little or no belly. This design allows it to cut through bones, meat, and hard and dense materials such as squash or pumpkin in a chopping motion. With a broad and heavy blade, the cleaver is also ideal for beating and pulverizing meat, poultry, fish, and crushing garlic.

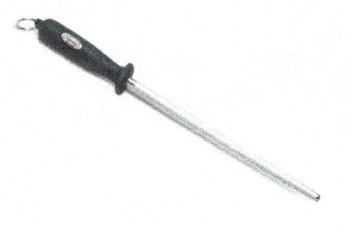

SHARPENING CERAMIC ROD/KNIFE SHARPENER

If you purchase a quality chef's knife (which you should), you'll want to take care of it so it lasts a lifetime. Maintaining a quality knife doesn't take many tools or much time. I would recommend a knife sharpener because it is safer than honing, which can be intimidating.

CUTTING BOARD

One primary tool you need in your kitchen is a good cutting board. You'll use it every time you cook (just like your chef's knife). There are various types of cutting boards—wood, plastic, and odor-resistant polypropylene are among the most popular. It's important to choose one that's durable and well-designed.

COOKWARE & BAKEWARE

SAUTÉ PAN

A sauté pan differs from a skillet in several important ways; it has a wide flat bottom and vertical sides that generally go up much higher than a skillet's flared sides. This makes cooking sauces, searing, and braising meat easier than in a skillet.

SMALL/MEDIUM SAUCEPAN

A lightweight and easy-to-handle saucepan is necessary when cooking small portions of soups, stews, pasta, or sauces. It's suitable for everything from boiling eggs to reheating leftover sauce or melting butter.

LARGE POT

You'll need a large pot to handle the volume when cooking large portions of soups, stews, pasta, or sauces.

CAST IRON SKILLET

Cast iron skillets have been workhorses in kitchens worldwide for more than 2,000 years. Modern skillets are made from heavy cast iron and pre-seasoned (so food doesn't stick). A 10-to-12-inch cast iron pot is relatively inexpensive for the stovetop and oven. The best way to keep your cast iron in good shape is to wash it by hand with little to no soap and blot it dry with a paper towel. Wipe your skillet with a paper towel dipped in vegetable oil to keep it in perfect condition.

BAKING SHEET

A sheet pan, baking tray, or baking sheet is a flat, rectangular metal pan used in an oven. It is often used for baking bread, pastries, roasting vegetables, and flat products such as cookies, sheet cakes, Swiss rolls, and pizzas.

BROILER PAN

A broiler pan is a rectangular metal pan for use under the high-heat broiler in the oven. Most of us find this pan in the drawer underneath the oven (which, if you did not know is a warming drawer). It is much thicker than a typical baking sheet pan, so it doesn't warp under the high heat and contains grooves and a draining pan that sits below to catch fat that drips through (so your oven doesn't get stained). Broiling is great when you want your food to get a nice brown crusty top.

CASSEROLE DISH

A casserole dish is a large, deep dish with high edges used for baking or serving. A quality casserole dish is a must for those lazy times you want to throw a one-dish meal into the oven (like lasagna or a casserole).

STOCK POT

A stock pot is ideally used to make stock or broth, which can be the basis for cooking more complex recipes. It is a wide pot with a flat bottom, straight sides, a wide opening to the full diameter of the pot, two handles on the sides, and a lid with a top handle.

OVEN MITTS

Oven mitts are used to protect your hands from being burned when transferring hot food to and from the oven. No longer will you have to wrap your hand in a tea towel and try not to spill your dish (or get burned) as you pull it out one-handed.

FOOD PROCESSOR

A food processor is a versatile kitchen appliance that can quickly and easily chop, slice, shred, grind, and puree almost any food. Some models can also assist the home cook in making citrus and vegetable juice, beating cake batter, kneading bread dough, beating egg whites, grinding meat, and slicing vegetables.

ELECTRIC MIXER

There are two basic types of mixers: stand or handheld. A mixer is a kitchen utensil that uses a gear-driven mechanism to rotate a set of beaters in a bowl. It automates the repetitive tasks of stirring, whisking, or beating. You will use this kitchen device more often when baking.

BASIC KITCHEN CONVERSIONS & EQUIVALENTS

DRY MEASUREMENTS CONVERSION CHART

3 teaspoons (tsp.) = 1 tablespoon (Tbsp.) = 1/16 cup

6 teaspoons = 2 tablespoons = 1/8 cup

12 teaspoons = 4 tablespoons = ¼ cup

24 teaspoons = 8 tablespoons = ½ cup

36 teaspoons = 12 tablespoons = ¾ cup

48 teaspoons = 16 tablespoons = 1 cup

LIQUID MEASUREMENTS CONVERSION CHART

8 fluid ounces (oz.) = 1 cup = ½ pint (pt.) = ¼ quart (qt.)

16 fluid ounces = 2 cups = 1 pint = ½ quart

32 fluid ounces = 4 cups = 2 pints = 1 quart = ¼ gallon (gal.)

128 fluid ounces = 16 cups = 8 pints = 4 quarts = 1 gallon

BUTTER

1 cup butter = 2 sticks = 8 ounces = 230 grams = 8 tablespoons

METRIC TO U.S. COOKING CONVERSIONS

Oven Temperatures

120 °C = 250 °F

160 °C = 320 °F

180 °C = 350 °F

205 °C = 400 °F

220 °C = 425 °F

Baking in Grams

1 cup flour = 140 grams

1 cup sugar = 150 grams

1 cup powdered sugar = 160 grams

1 cup heavy cream = 235 grams

Volume

1 milliliter = 1/5 teaspoon

5 ml. = 1 teaspoon

15 ml. = 1 tablespoon

240 ml. = 1 cup or 8 fluid ounces

1 liter = 34 fl. ounces

Weight

1 gram = .035 ounces

100 grams = 3.5 ounces

500 grams = 1.1 pounds

1 kilogram = 35 ounces

U.S. TO METRIC COOKING CONVERSIONS

1 CUP EQUIVALENTS

1 cup = 8 fluid ounces

1 cup = 16 tablespoons

1 cup = 48 teaspoons

1 cup = ½ pint

1 cup = ¼ quart

1 cup = 1/16 gallon

1 cup = 240 ml.

BAKING PAN EQUIVALENTS

9-inch Round Cake Pan = 12 cups

10- inch Tube Pan =16 cups

10- inch Bundt Pan = 12 cups

9- inch Springform Pan = 10 cups

9 X 5 inch Loaf Pan= 8 cups

9- inch Square Pan = 8 cups

1/5 tsp. = 1 ml.

1 tsp. = 5 ml.

1 Tbsp.= 15 ml.

1 fl. ounce = 30 ml.

1 cup = 237 ml.

1 pint (2 cups) = 473 ml.

1 quart (4 cups) = .95 liter

1 gallon (16 cups) = 3.8 liters

1 oz. = 28 grams

1 pound = 454 grams

BAKING EQUIVALENTS

1 cup all-purpose flour = 4.5 oz.

1 cup rolled oats = 3 oz.

1 large egg = 1.7 oz.

1 cup butter = 8 oz.

1 cup milk = 8 oz.

1 cup heavy cream = 8.4 oz

1 cup granulated sugar = 7.1 oz.

1 cup packed brown sugar = 7.75 oz.

1 cup vegetable oil = 7.7 oz.

1 cup unsifted powdered sugar = 4.4 oz.

BASIC KITCHEN KNIFE CUTS

BATON (CUT CHIPS)

Thick-cut chips or steak fries are cut in chunky batons about 8 mm. in thickness. This is the largest stick cut and the intermediate step for the medium dice. Recipes for chunky stews often call for carrots, potatoes, and meat to be medium diced, which you get after you chop up the batons into cubes. The large dice (2 cm. cube) are not commonly used in cooking, but you might use a large dice for watermelon.

BATONNET (FRENCH FRY CUT)

For dipping, some common foods cut in this style are French fries and crudites (or vegetable sticks). To cut your vegetables into batonnets, square them off, then cut lengthwise into 6 mm. thin rectangular slices before cutting them into 6 mm. sticks. If a recipe for something like minestrone calls for a small dice, first cut the vegetables into batonnets, then chop them down further into 6 mm. cubes.

JULIENNE (MATCHSTICK CUTS)

The julienne is also known as the matchstick cut. As its name suggests, you're going for a thin, stick-shaped cut. To make a julienne cut, square off your vegetable, then cut lengthwise into 3 mm. thin rectangular slices. Then cut these slices into matchsticks. This cut is commonly used for stir-fries, as ingredients cut this way cook evenly and quickly.

BRUNOISE (FINE DICE)

The brunoise is the finest dice and is derived from the julienne. Any smaller cut will be considered a mince. To brunoise, gather the julienned vegetable strips together, then dice them into even 3 mm. cubes. This cut is most often used for making sauces like crushed tomato or as an aromatic garnish on dishes.

CHIFFONADE (SHREDDING)

Unlike all the cuts mentioned above, which are used for larger, hard vegetables, the chiffonade is a cut that's applied to herbs and leafy vegetables. A finer chiffonade achieves thin ribbons of herbs for garnishing, while a larger chiffonade can be used on leafy greens for a sauté. To chiffonade, stack all the leaves together and roll them tightly, holding them down with one hand and slicing the leaves perpendicular to the roll.

MACEDOINE (LARGE DICE)

This technique is used to cut vegetables and fruit into large cubes, which is ideal for preparing vegetables that will be used in soups. Chefs also cut melons and other types of large fruit utilizing this technique. When making large dice, it is crucial to make your cuts on a flat surface.

KITCHEN TERMINOLOGY (FROM A TO Z)

AL DENTE:

Italian term is used to describe pasta cooked until it offers a slight resistance to the bite.

BAKE:

To cook by dry heat, usually in the oven.

BARBECUE:

In general terms, barbecue is grilling outdoors or over an open charcoal or wood fire. More specifically, barbecue refers to long, slow, direct-heat cooking, including liberal basting with a barbecue sauce.

BASTE:

To moisten foods during cooking with pan drippings or special sauce to add flavor and prevent drying.

BATTER:

A mixture containing flour and liquid, thin enough to pour.

BEAT:

To mix rapidly to make a mixture smooth and light by incorporating as much air as possible.

BLANCH:

To immerse in rapidly boiling water and allow to cook slightly.

BLEND:

To incorporate two or more ingredients thoroughly.

BOIL:

To heat a liquid until bubbles break continually on the surface.

BROIL:

To cook on a grill under strong, direct heat.

CARAMELIZE:

To heat sugar in order to turn it brown and give it a special taste.

CHOP:

To cut solids into pieces using a sharp knife or another chopping device.

CLARIFY:

To separate and remove solids from a liquid, thus making it clear.

CREAM:

To soften fat, especially butter, by beating it at room temperature. Butter and sugar are often creamed together, making a smooth, soft paste.

CURE:

To preserve meats by drying and salting, and/or smoking.

DEGLAZE:

To dissolve the thin glaze of juices and brown bits on the surface of a pan in which food has been fried, sauteed, or roasted. To do this, add liquid and stir and scrape over high heat, thereby adding flavor to the liquid for use as a sauce.

DEGREASE:

To remove fat from the surface of stews, soups, or stock. The fat is usually cooled in the refrigerator until it hardens and can be easily removed.

DICE:

To cut food into small cubes of uniform size and shape.

DISSOLVE:

To cause a dry substance to become incorporated into a liquid forming a solution.

DREDGE:

To sprinkle or coat with flour or other fine substances.

DRIZZLE:

To sprinkle drops of liquid lightly over food in a casual manner.

DUST:

To sprinkle food with dry ingredients. Use a strainer or a jar with a perforated cover, or try the good, old-fashioned way and shake things together in a paper bag.

FILLET OR FILET:

As a verb, it is to remove the bones from meat or fish. As a noun, it is the piece of flesh that remains after the meat or fish has been boned (had the bones removed).

FLAKE:

To break lightly into small pieces.

FLAMBE':

To flame foods by dousing them in some form of potable alcohol and setting them alight.

FOLD:

To incorporate a delicate substance, such as whipped cream or beaten egg whites, into another substance without releasing air bubbles. Cut down through the mixture with a spoon, whisk, or fork; go across the bottom of the bowl, up and over, close to the surface. The process is repeated while slowly rotating the bowl until the ingredients are thoroughly blended.

FRICASSEE:

To cook by braising; usually applied to fowl or rabbit.

FRY:

To cook in hot fat. Cooking in a fat is called pan-frying or sauteing; cooking in a one-to-two-inch layer of hot fat is called shallow-fat frying; cooking in a deep layer of hot fat is called deep-fat frying.

GARNISH:

To decorate a dish both to enhance its appearance and to provide a flavorful foil. Parsley, lemon slices, raw vegetables, chopped chives, and other herbs are all forms of garnishes.

GLAZE:

To cook with a thin sugar syrup cooked to crack stage; mixture may be thickened slightly. Glaze also means to cover with a thin, glossy icing.

GRATE:

To rub on a grater that separates the food in various sizes of bits or shreds.

GRATIN:

From the French word for "crust." A term used to describe any oven-baked dish—usually cooked in a shallow oval gratin dish—on which a golden-brown crust of breadcrumbs, cheese, or creamy sauce is formed.

GRILL:

To cook on a grill over intense heat.

GRIND:

To process solids by hand or mechanically to reduce them to tiny particles.

JULIENNE:

To cut vegetables, fruits, or cheeses into thin strips.

KNEAD:

To work and press dough with the palms of the hands or mechanically to develop the gluten in the flour.

LUKEWARM:

Neither cool nor warm; approximately body temperature.

MARINATE:

To flavor and moisturize pieces of meat, poultry, seafood, or vegetables by soaking them in or brushing them with a liquid mixture of seasonings known as a marinade. Dry marinade mixtures composed of salt, pepper, herbs, or spices may also be rubbed into meat, poultry, or seafood.

MEUNIERE:

Dredged with flour and sauteed in butter.

MINCE:

To cut or chop food into extremely small pieces.

MISE EN PLACE:

The preparation of ingredients before cooking begins, for example, dicing onions or measuring spices.

MIX:

To combine ingredients usually by stirring.

PAN-BROIL:

To cook uncovered in a hot fry pan, pouring off fat as it accumulates.

PAN-FRY:

To cook in small amounts of fat.

PARBOIL:

To boil until partially cooked or to blanch. Usually, this procedure is followed by final cooking in a seasoned sauce.

PARE:

To remove the outermost skin of a fruit or vegetable.

PEEL:

To remove the peels from vegetables or fruits.

PICKLE:

To preserve meats, vegetables, and fruits in brine.

PINCH:

A pinch is the trifling amount you can hold between your thumb and forefinger.

PIT:

To remove pits from fruits.

PLANKED:

Cooked on a thick hardwood plank.

PLUMP:

To soak dried fruits in liquid until they swell.

POACH:

To cook very gently in hot liquid kept just below the boiling point.

PUREE:

To mash foods until perfectly smooth by hand, by rubbing through a sieve or food mill, or by whirling in a blender or food processor.

REDUCE:

To boil down to reduce the volume.

REFRESH:

To run cold water over food that has been parboiled, to stop the cooking process quickly.

RENDER:

To make solid fat into liquid by melting it slowly.

ROAST:

To cook by dry heat in an oven.

SAUTÉ:

To cook and/or brown food in a small amount of hot fat.

SCALD:

To bring to a temperature just below the boiling point.

SCALLOP:

To bake a food, usually in a casserole, with sauce or other liquid. Crumbs often are sprinkled over the top of the dish.

SCORE:

To cut narrow grooves or gashes partway through the outer surface of food.

SEAR:

To brown very quickly by intense heat. This method increases shrinkage but develops flavor and improves appearance.

SHRED:

To cut or tear in small, long, narrow pieces.

SIFT:

To put one or more dry ingredients through a sieve or sifter.

SIMMER:

To cook slowly in liquid over low heat at a temperature of about 180°. The surface of the liquid should be barely moving, broken from time to time by slowly rising bubbles.

SKIM:

To remove impurities, whether scum or fat, from the surface of a liquid during cooking, thereby resulting in a clear, cleaner-tasting final produce.

STEAM:

To cook in steam in a pressure cooker, deep-well cooker, double boiler, or a steamer made by fitting a rack in a kettle with a tight cover. A small amount of boiling water is used, and more water is added during the steaming process, if necessary.

STEEP:

To extract color, flavor, or other qualities from a substance by leaving it in water just below the boiling point.

STERILIZE:

To destroy microorganisms by boiling, dry heat, or steam.

STEW:

To simmer slowly in a small amount of liquid for a long time.

STIR:

To mix ingredients with a circular motion until well blended or of uniform consistency.

TOSS:

To combine ingredients with a lifting motion.

TRUSS:

To secure poultry with string or skewers to hold its shape while cooking.

WHIP:

To beat rapidly to incorporate air and produce expansion, as in heavy cream or egg whites.

COOKING INTERNAL TEMPERATURE CHART

MINIMUM INTERNAL TEMPERATURE & REST TIME

Beef, Pork, Veal & Lamb

Steaks, chops, roasts

145 °F (62.8 °C) and allow to rest for at least 3 minutes

Ground Meats

160 °F (71.1 °C)

Ham, fresh or smoked (uncooked)

145 °F (62.8 °C) and allow to rest for at least 3 minutes

Fully Cooked Ham

Reheat cooked hams packaged in USDA-inspected plants to 140 °F (60 °C) and all others to 165 °F (73.9 °C)

MINIMUM INTERNAL TEMPERATURE

Poultry Breasts, whole bird, legs, thighs, wings, giblets, and stuffing	165 °F (73.9 °C)
Ground Poultry	165 °F (73.89 °C)
Eggs	160 °F (71.1 °C)
Fish & Shellfish	145 °F (62.8 °C)
Leftovers	165 °F (73.9 °C)
Casseroles	165 °F (73.9 °C)

NEXT

SOUPS, SALADS & SANDWICHES

AT HOME WITH
Chef Mark Phillips

SOUPS, SALADS & SANDWICHES

When people ask me, "What is your favorite food?" I say that I am completely content with a sandwich, salad, and/or soup. It is like the adage, "the shoemaker wears the worst shoes." I am like that with food for myself sometimes. Yes, I love to cook lavish meals and create some of the most intricate plating decorations, but the simplicity of "The 3 Ss" brings me so much joy. My friends and family look forward to the fall and winter because they know soups made from scratch are on the way.

Soups are comfort foods that gather richness through a layering process of flavors that mature over time as they boil together and reduce into yummy goodness. Soup is thought to be as old as the history of cooking with the first evidence of soup making going as far back as 20,000 B.C. Soup's simplicity makes it an ideal meal for hard times when food is scarce, and ingredients are limited. I want to teach you to make some of my most popular soups from the classic chicken noodle soup to my famous crab and corn chowder. The layering of flavors creates a liquid party in your mouth.

People may think of salads as healthy choices or as lacking in flavor, but one can get highly creative in the salad department. Salad can be an entree, or a side dish prepared and composed of a mixture of ingredients and intended to be eaten cold. The ingredients in salads could be vegetables, pasta, beans, seafood, tuna, eggs, chicken, fruit, rice, and even jello. I have put together a couple of my favorite salads for you to try at home—some with lettuce and others not so much.

Good quality bread elevates any sandwich. Whether you are having a simple turkey sandwich or aged thinly sliced prosciutto with buffalo mozzarella, choose quality over quantity. The sandwich is of British origin. It was intended to be a small handheld snack where one's hand would not get dirty. Like most food genres, sandwiches have their own day—November 3rd is National Sandwich Day.

If you are like me and sometimes get bored with the same ole soup, salad, or sandwich, why not make it fun? I hope these recipes inspire you to try out a recipe and even add your own twist. You really can't go wrong with this section. You can keep it simple or go all out, the choice is yours. Grab your stock pot, greens, and a fresh loaf of bread, and let's have some fun!

CRAB & CORN CHOWDER

SERVINGS: 4-6 | PREP: 10 MINS | TOTAL: 30 MINS

INGREDIENTS

1 tablespoon olive oil

2 tablespoons butter

2 russet potatoes, skin on and diced

1 red bell pepper, seeded and diced

1 green bell pepper, seeded and diced

1 medium onion, diced

2 tablespoons chopped thyme

1 dried bay leaf

salt and black pepper, to taste

2 tablespoons Blackened Redfish Seasoning

3 tablespoons all-purpose flour

2 cups vegetable or chicken stock

1 quart heavy cream

3 cups fresh corn kernels, cut from the cob

8 ounces crab claw meat

DIRECTIONS

1. Heat the oil and butter in a deep pot over medium heat.
2. Add them to the pot as you chop the vegetables (potatoes, bell peppers, onion). Add the chopped thyme and bay leaf to the pot.
3. Season the vegetables with salt and pepper to taste, and add the Blackened Red Fish Seasoning. Sauté the vegetables for 5 minutes.
4. Sprinkle in the flour and cook for a further 2 minutes, stirring constantly. Add the chicken broth and stir well to combine.
5. Stir in the heavy cream and combine. Bring the soup up to a bubble. Add the corn and crab meat and simmer for 7 minutes.
6. Taste the soup and adjust the seasoning. Remove the bay leaf.
7. Ladle the soup into bread bowls or soup bowls, and garnish with oyster crackers, sliced scallions or toasted French bread.

OPTIONAL GARNISHES

oyster crackers

scallion, sliced

French bread, toasted

CHEF NOTES

Soup will last 3-4 days in the refrigerator and 4-6 months in the freezer.

CHICKEN TOSCANA

SERVINGS: 8 | PREP: 10 MINS | TOTAL: 45 MINS

INGREDIENTS

2 spicy Italian chicken sausage links; skin removed & cut into 1-inch chunks

2 sweet Italian chicken sausage links; skin removed medium chucks

½ large onion, diced

2-3 cloves of garlic, minced

32 oz (4 cups) low-sodium chicken broth

2 cups water

5 medium russet potatoes; medium dice

1 teaspoon crushed red pepper flakes (optional)

salt and pepper, to taste

4 cups chopped kale

1 ½ cup heavy whipping cream

Parmesan cheese, grated (optional)

DIRECTIONS

1. Brown the sausages in a large pot or Dutch oven. Remove sausage with a slotted spoon and set aside. Stir in the chopped onion and cook for 5 - 6 minutes, or until the onion is translucent. Stir in the minced garlic and cook for a further 1 minute, stirring frequently.

2. Add the chicken broth and water to the pot. Stir in the red pepper flakes and salt and pepper to taste.

3. Add the potatoes and sausage to the pot and bring to a simmer over medium heat. Continue to cook until the potatoes are tender, about 10 minutes.

4. Add the kale to the soup and simmer for a further 5 - 10 minutes, stirring occasionally. Stir in the heavy cream and heat through for another 5 - 7 minutes.

5. Ladle soup into bowls and (optional) serve with Parmesan cheese.

HERBED CHICKEN NOODLE SOUP

SERVINGS: 6 | PREP: 15 MINS | TOTAL: 35 MINS

INGREDIENTS

2 tablespoons olive oil

2 cloves garlic, finely chopped

1 cup diced celery

8 medium green onions, sliced (½ cup)

2 medium carrots, chopped (1 cup)

3 springs of thyme

1 teaspoon sage

2 cups cubed cooked chicken (rotisserie chicken or cooked chicken breast)

2 cups uncooked egg noodles (5 oz)

1 tablespoon chopped fresh parsley or 1 teaspoon dried parsley

¼ teaspoon pepper

1 dried bay leaf

6 cups chicken broth

DIRECTIONS

1. Heat oil in a 3-quart saucepan over medium heat. Add the garlic, celery, onions, carrots, thyme, and sage, and cook 4 minutes, stirring occasionally.

2. Stir in all the remaining ingredients. Bring to the boil; and then reduce the heat. Cover and simmer for about 10 minutes, stirring occasionally, until the carrots and noodles are tender. Remove the bay leaf.

CHEF NOTES

Pasta continues to absorb liquid, so if you are making the soup ahead of time, skip adding the noodles. Cook the noodles separately and stir them in just before serving.

If you prefer, you can substitute the egg noodles with rotini, fusilli, or cavatappi pasta for a change of pace.

Refrigerate soup in a shallow, wide container, so they cool more rapidly. Once completely cooled, cover tightly and refrigerate. Refrigerate most soups that contain vegetables or meat for no more than 3 days. You can freeze soup for up to 6 months but leave about a ½ inch of space between the top of the soup and the lid.

SAGE ROASTED BUTTERNUT SQUASH SOUP

SERVINGS: 4 TO 6 | PREP: 10 MINS | TOTAL: 55 MINS

INGREDIENTS

1 large butternut squash, halved and de-seeded; cut into large cubes

1 tablespoon olive oil, plus more for drizzling

¼ cup chopped sweet onion

½ cup chopped shallot (about 1 large shallot bulb)

4 garlic cloves, pressed or minced

2-3 teaspoons chopped sage

1 teaspoon salt

24 - 32 ounces vegetable broth, as needed

1 teaspoon brown sugar

☒ teaspoon ground nutmeg

freshly ground black pepper, to taste

24 - 32 ounces vegetable broth, as needed

1 to 2 tablespoons butter, to taste

DIRECTIONS

1. Preheat the oven to 425° F. Line a baking sheet with parchment paper.

2. Place the diced butternut squash and chopped sweet onions on the baking sheets. Lightly coat with olive oil, and season with salt and pepper. Roast in the oven for 30-40 minutes. When done, remove from the oven and set aside until it's cool enough to handle about 10 minutes.

3. Meanwhile, in a large pot, warm 1 tablespoon olive oil over medium heat until oil is shimmering. Add chopped shallots, sage and 1 teaspoon salt. Cook the shallots and sage, stirring until the onions are translucent and have golden edges, about 3 to 4 minutes. Add the garlic and cook for a further minute, stirring frequently.

4. Add the vegetable broth to the pot and bring to a low simmer. To a blender add the roasted butternut squash, brown sugar, nutmeg, and a few twists of freshly ground black pepper. Ladle approximately 3 cups of stock to the blender (be careful with the hot liquid). Do not fill the blender jug past the maximum fill line. Securely fasten the lid and blend on medium-high until the soup has a creamy texture. Be careful about the hot steam escaping from the lid.

5. If you prefer, you can thin the soup by adding more of the remaining stock. Transfer the soup back to the pot over low heat. Add 1 or 2 tablespoons butter to taste. To keep the soup dairy-free substitute the butter with olive oil. Taste and adjust the seasoning with salt and pepper if needed.

6. Ladle the soup into bowls and serve. I like to top mine off with a little freshly ground black pepper.

CHEF NOTES

Preparing a butternut squash can be intimidating, so I wanted to share a few tips on how to cut a squash safely. You'll need a sharp knife and a non-slip cutting board. Place a damp towel underneath for added security and stability. Cut off the top (just under the stem) and the very bottom of the squash. Stand the squash upright on the base that has been cut flat and (carefully) cut the squash in half. Remove the seeds with a large spoon. Lay the squash cut-side down on the board and, using a peeler remove the skin. When the skin has been removed, cut into large cubes.

Allow any leftover soup cool to room temperature before transferring to a storage container and refrigerating. Keep in the fridge for up to 4 days or in the freezer for 4 months.

KALE & QUINOA GREEK SALAD

SERVINGS: 6-8 | PREP: 15 MINS | TOTAL: 25 MINS

INGREDIENTS

¾ cup tri-colored quinoa

1 bunch of kale, leaves removed from the stems and shredded

½ cup finely diced red onion

½ cup diced English cucumber

½ cup grape tomatoes, halved

¼ cup sliced pitted kalamata olives

3 oz feta cheese, crumbled

FOR THE DRESSING

1 garlic clove, minced

1 small shallot, finely diced

juice of 1 lemon

2 tablespoons extra-virgin olive oil

1 teaspoon maple syrup

2 teaspoons Dijon mustard

1 teaspoon red wine vinegar

kosher salt, to taste

freshly cracked pepper, to taste

DIRECTIONS

1. Rinse the quinoa well with water. Add to a saucepan along with 1⅓ cups of water and bring to a boil. Cover, reduce the heat to medium-low, and simmer for 15- 20 minutes until the quinoa is done.

2. In the meantime, prepare the dressing. Add all the dressing ingredients to a bowl and whisk together. This will soften the shallots and allow the flavors to come together.

3. To a large bowl, add the chopped kale and half of the dressing. Gently massage the dressing into the kale for 3-4 minutes. Add the quinoa, red onion, olives, cucumber, tomatoes, olives, and half of the feta and toss the ingredients together.

4. Garish with the remaining feta and extra dressing if desired.

ASIAN-STYLE CHICKEN CHOPPED SALAD

SERVINGS: 4 TO 6 | PREP: 15 MINS | TOTAL: 15 MINS

INGREDIENTS

4 cups shredded cabbage

1 cup shredded red cabbage

¼ cup shredded carrots

¼ cup edamame

½ red bell pepper, thinly sliced

1 cup cooked chicken breast, thinly sliced

¼ cup toasted almonds or roasted cashews

2 green onions, finely sliced

FOR THE DRESSING

2 tablespoons light soy sauce

½ cup olive oil

3 tablespoons rice wine vinegar

1 tablespoon sesame oil

1 tablespoon fresh lime juice

1 garlic clove, minced

1 ½ tablespoon minced fresh ginger

1 tablespoon toasted sesame seeds

2 tablespoons water

DIRECTIONS

1. Add all the dressing ingredients to a bowl and whisk to combine. Alternatively, add the ingredients to a jar and vigorously shake to combine. For increased flavor, make the dressing an hour before needed.

2. If you want a smoother and creamier dressing, add all the ingredients to a food processor or blender and process until smooth and creamy.

3. Toss all the salad ingredients together in a large bowl. It is best to add the dressing to the salad just before serving; otherwise, the salad may become soggy.

ARUGULA, MOZZARELLA & TORTELLINI SALAD

SERVINGS: 4 | PREP: 15 MINS | TOTAL: 15 MINS

INGREDIENTS

1 cup cooked cheese tortellini

½ cup basil pesto (see recipe on page 65)

1 cup cherry tomatoes; halved

¼ cup chopped red onion (optional)

3 cups arugula leaves

1 cup baby mozzarella

balsamic glaze or reduction

Prosciutto (optional)

1 tablespoon chopped fresh basil

DIRECTIONS

1. Bring a large pot of salted water to a rolling boil. Add the tortellini and cook for 1 ½ minute less than the package instructions. Drain and rinse with cold water. Allow to drain again.

2. Place the tortellini in a large bowl, add the pesto, tomatoes and onions, and toss together.

3. When ready to serve, add the arugula and baby mozzarella and toss together with the tortellini.

4. Drizzle balsamic glaze over the salad and top with chopped basil and (optional) Prosciutto.

CHEF NOTES

This salad can be prepared in advance however I would only add the arugula when ready to serve as it will wilt after a short period of time is it sits for too long.

ROSEMARY FRIED CHICKEN & AVOCADO COBB SALAD

SERVINGS: 4 TO 6 | PREP: 20 MINS | TOTAL: 55 MINS

INGREDIENTS

FOR CHICKEN TENDERS

1-2 pounds chicken tenders or 2 large boneless skinless chicken breasts, sliced into 1-inch strips

1 cup all-purpose flour

½ cup corn starch

1 teaspoon dried rosemary

1 teaspoon onion powder

1 teaspoon garlic powder

¾ teaspoon salt

½ teaspoon black pepper

2 egg whites, beaten

vegetable oil for frying

FOR THE SALAD

4-6 slices cooked bacon, rough chopped

1 head romaine, roughly chopped

6 cherry tomatoes, cut into quarters

1 avocado, halved, peeled, deseeded, peeled and sliced

½ small red onion, thinly sliced

4-6 soft-boiled eggs, peeled and halved

¼ cup roasted corn

¼ cup shredded cheddar cheese

croutons (optional)

FOR THE RANCH DRESSING:

¼ cup mayonnaise

½ cup sour cream

½ cup buttermilk

1 teaspoon salt

¼ teaspoon cracked pepper

¼ teaspoon garlic powder

¼ teaspoon onion powder

½ teaspoon chives

☒ teaspoon parsley

½ teaspoon dill

1-2 teaspoons lemon juice, to taste

CHEF NOTES

For those watching your figure, you can replace the fried chicken with grilled or baked chicken for a healthier option. You can remove the bacon and chicken to make this a vegetarian salad. You can even add grilled shrimp or steak, it's up to you!

DIRECTIONS

FOR THE RANCH DRESSING

Whisk together the mayonnaise, sour cream, and buttermilk in a medium-sized bowl until smooth. Add salt, pepper, garlic powder, onion powder, chives, parsley, dill and lemon juice and whisk until smooth. Taste and adjust the salt if necessary. Cover and refrigerate for 30 – 60 minutes before using.

FOR THE FRIED CHICKEN

1. Fill a deep, heavy-bottomed pot or cast-iron skillet with about 4 inches of oil. Heat over medium-high heat while you flour the chicken. Keep an eye on the oil because you do not want it to burn.

2. In a large bowl, mix the flour, corn starch, rosemary, onion powder, garlic powder, salt, and pepper. In another bowl, beat the egg whites.

3. Dredge the chicken in the flour mixture, coating well. Shake off excess flour, dip into the egg whites, and then back into the flour. Place the chicken on a tray and leave it to rest for a few minutes before frying. Repeat with the remaining chicken.

4. If you have a candy thermometer, check the temperature of the oil. You want it to be 350 – 370° F. Alternatively, if you don't have a thermometer, dip the handle of a wooden spoon in the oil, and if bubbles form around the handle, your oil is ready. Fry 5-7 pieces of chicken at a time until golden brown, about 5-7 minutes per side. Transfer to a paper towel-lined plate to drain excess oil. Repeat with the remaining chicken. Sprinkle with a little more salt if needed.

FOR THE SALAD

On a large platter, spread out the lettuce and then add rows of hardboiled egg, chicken, bacon, avocado, onion, cheddar cheese, and cherry tomatoes. Add the croutons (optional).

WATERMELON, FETA & MINT SALAD

SERVINGS: 4 | PREP: 10 MINS | TOTAL: 10 MINS

INGREDIENTS

3 cups cubed watermelon, seeded

1 ½ cups sliced English cucumber, seeded

2 tablespoons mint, thinly sliced (or small mint leaves)

3 tablespoons olive oil

1 tablespoon lime juice

salt and pepper, to taste

½ cup feta cheese, crumbled

pumpkin seeds, toasted (optional)

DIRECTIONS

1. Place the watermelon, cucumber, and mint in a large bowl. In a small bowl, whisk together the olive oil, lime juice and salt and pepper to taste.

2. Drizzle the dressing over the melon salad and toss to coat.

3. Scatter over the feta and (optional) pumpkin seeds and serve.

DIRECTIONS

1. Mix all the remoulade ingredients in a medium size bowl. Chill in the refrigerator while you make the rest of the sandwich.

2. Mix the salt, cayenne pepper, black pepper, garlic powder, and onion powder in a bowl. In another bowl mix the all-purpose flour and corn meal. Add half of the seasoning and mix it with the flour mixture.

3. Add the shrimp to a bowl and sprinkle over the remaining seasoning mixture. Pour over the hot sauce and buttermilk and toss lightly to coat the shrimp.

4. Pour 3 inches of oil into a heavy-bottomed pot and heat to 350° F. Prepare a wire rack by lining it with a few layers of paper towel. Have the vegetables and bread for the sandwich prepared in advance. You want everything ready so you can serve the shrimp as soon as they are done.

5. Dip the prepared shrimp into the flour mixture and shake off any excess.

6. Cooking in batches, fry the coated shrimp until golden brown, about 3-5 minutes. Transfer to the paper-lined racks to drain excess oil.

7. Time to assemble the Po'boy! Build the sandwich by first spreading with remoulade and then dressing with lettuce, tomato and pickles. Pile on the shrimp and then finish with some more remoulade and a drizzle of hot sauce.

8. Serve immediately.

FRIED SHRIMP PO'BOY

SERVINGS: 4 | PREP: 15 MINS | TOTAL: 40 MINS

INGREDIENTS

FOR THE REMOULADE

½ cup mayonnaise

2 teaspoon grain or Dijon mustard

1 tablespoon capers, chopped

1 teaspoon hot sauce (e.g. Texas Pete)

1 ½ teaspoons paprika

2 teaspoons lemon juice

1 garlic clove, minced

FOR THE FRIED SHRIMP

1 ½ pounds raw, medium shrimp (21-25 size)

1 ½ teaspoons salt

½ teaspoon cayenne pepper

½ teaspoon black pepper

1 teaspoon garlic powder

½ teaspoon onion powder

1 cup all-purpose flour

1 cup corn meal

½ cup buttermilk

1 tablespoon hot sauce

1 tomato sliced

1 cup shredded lettuce

dill pickles for garnish

4 (8 inch) French loaves, split horizontally

CHEF NOTES

This sandwich can also be done with grilled or sautéed shrimp instead of deep-fried. You would use the same seasoning but you skip the buttermilk and dipping into flour steps. Sauté the shrimp on medium-high heat for 3-5 minutes on each side and finish the Po'boy the same way

GRILLED PORTABELLA MUSHROOM CAPRESE PANINI

SERVINGS: 2-4 | PREP: 15 MINS | TOTAL: 35 MINS

INGREDIENTS

2 large portobello mushrooms, stems removed & sliced horizontally into 2 thin pieces

1 roasted red pepper, seeds and ribs removed

1-2 tablespoons olive oil

kosher salt and freshly ground black pepper

½ cup spinach

1 loaf of French bread

4-6 slices provolone cheese

Balsamic glaze

2-4 slices prosciutto

1 tablespoon basil pesto(optional or see recipe on page 65)

DIRECTIONS

1. Heat a grill pan to medium-high heat. On a sheet pan, rub the mushrooms with olive oil and sprinkle with salt and pepper. Toss to coat. Grill the portobellos for 3 minutes per side, 6 minutes total. Place roasted red pepper on top of the mushroom and grill for another 3 minutes. Remove from the grill, add cheese and set aside until cool enough to handle.

2. Cut two 4-inch pieces of bread, then slice in half lengthwise. Pile on the grilled portobellos, red peppers, and spinach on 2 slices of the bread, drizzle balsamic and prosciutto and close the sandwiches. (If using basil pesto, you would spread it on the bread at the beginning of step 2)

3. Place the sandwiches on top of the hot grill pan and place a cast-iron skillet on top to press. Cook for 3 to 4 minutes, then flip and cook 3 to 4 more minutes on the remaining side. Slice on a diagonal and serve.

JIBARITO "PLANTAIN" SANDWICH

SERVINGS: 1 | PREP: 10 MINS | TOTAL: 25 MINS

INGREDIENTS

1 tablespoon mayonnaise

1 teaspoon lime juice

1 teaspoon chopped cilantro

pinch of salt

2 cups vegetable oil for frying

1 green plantain, peeled and halved lengthwise

2 tablespoons vegetable oil

4 ounces beef skirt steak or grilled chicken, cut into thin strips

¼ medium yellow onion, thinly sliced

1 clove of garlic, minced

pinch of cumin

pinch of dried oregano

2 slices tomato

3 lettuce leaves

DIRECTIONS

1. To a small bowl add the mayonnaise, lime juice, cilantro, and a pinch of salt. Whisk together and place in the refrigerator.

2. Heat 2 cups of vegetable oil in a large, deep skillet to 350° F (or use a deep fryer if you have one). When the oil is hot, fry the plantain halves for 1 to 2 minutes, or until they float. Remove from the oil and drain on paper towels.

3. Place the par-cooked plantain halves between 2 cutting boards and firmly press down to flatten them. Fry the flattened plantains for another 2-3 minutes until golden brown. Remove from the oil and drain on paper towels.

4. Heat 2 tablespoons of oil in a large skillet over medium-high heat. Add the skirt steak (or chicken), onion, garlic, cumin, and oregano. Cook, frequently stirring, until the steak is cooked to your liking.

5. To serve, spread the mayonnaise mixture on one of the plantain slices. Top with the steak and onion mixture, lettuce, and tomato. Place the other plantain half on top to form a sandwich. Cut in half and serve.

CHEF NOTES

If you choose to use chicken, follow the same steps as for the steak. Be sure to cook the chicken until done (internal temperature of 165° F).

You can add cheese to the sandwich to add some extra tasty goodness! I recommend Swiss or American.

I discovered this traditional Puerto Rican sandwich when I was living in Miami. A good thing about this sandwich is that it has no bread, so it's a good alternative for people with gluten allergies.

LOBSTER ROLLS

SERVINGS: 4 | PREP: 20 MINS | TOTAL: 30 MINS

INGREDIENTS

1-pound cooked lobster meat, cut into bite-sized chunks

½ cup mayonnaise

2 teaspoons fresh lemon juice

¼ cup finely chopped celery

1 teaspoon chopped fresh parsley

2 teaspoons green tops from a scallion, finely minced

dash of hot sauce, to taste

1 teaspoon Old Bay Seasoning

freshly ground black pepper (a few grinds or to taste)

4 split-top Hawaiian rolls (or brioche bun)

2 tablespoons melted butter

DIRECTIONS

1. Place the cooked lobster meat into a large bowl.
2. In another smaller bowl, combine the mayonnaise, lemon juice, celery, parsley, scallion, hot sauce, Old Bay Seasoning, and black pepper. Mix and taste for seasoning. If necessary, adjust the seasoning until you have it to your liking. Add to the lobster meat and mix well.
3. Brush both sides of the rolls with butter. Toast both sides in a medium frying pan over medium heat until nicely browned.
4. Divide the lobster salad between the rolls. If you prefer, add some lettuce to the rolls before adding the lobster. It's your choice; we like it without lettuce.

HERB DE PROVENCE CHICKEN SALAD CROISSANT SANDWICH

SERVINGS: 4-6 | PREP: 10 MINS | TOTAL: 30 MINS

INGREDIENTS

2 boneless, skinless chicken breasts

1 tablespoon olive oil

salt and pepper, to taste

1 tablespoon herb de Provence

2 teaspoons onion powder

2 teaspoons garlic powder

½ -1 cup mayonnaise

2 teaspoons tarragon vinegar (or rice wine vinegar)

1 bunch basil; chopped

1 medium onion; diced

4 croissant rolls

leafy lettuce

sliced tomatoes

DIRECTIONS

1. Preheat oven to 375° F.

2. Take a large piece of aluminum foil and place the chicken breasts in the middle. Season both sides of the chicken breasts with olive oil, salt, pepper, herb de Provence, onion powder, and garlic powder. Bring the edges of the foil together and fold to seal and make a pouch. Place on a tray and bake in the oven for 20 minutes. Remove from the oven, carefully open the pouch and set aside to cool for approximately 20 mins. Reserve the cooking juices in the foil pouch. Shred chicken using two forks, or if you prefer, you can roughly chop the chicken.

3. To a medium-sized mixing bowl, add mayo, vinegar, and basil. Add the shredded chicken and diced onion and mix well. At this stage you can add 1 to 2 teaspoons of the reserved cooking juice to the chicken mixture for added flavor and/or make the chicken salad moister.

4. You can serve it immediately on a toasted croissant or, like me, let the chicken salad rest in the refrigerator for at least one hour for the flavors to blend.

5. Serve with lettuce and sliced tomatoes, and enjoy!

BASIL PESTO

YIELD: ½ CUP

INGREDIENTS

3 cups fresh basil leaves, lightly packed

⅓ cup grated parmesan cheese

2-3 cloves garlic, minced

1 teaspoon lemon zest

¼ cup pine nuts, toasted (see notes)

2 teaspoons lemon juice

½ cup olive oil

DIRECTIONS

1. Add the basil leaves, parmesan cheese, minced garlic, lemon zest, pine nuts, and lemon juice to a blender or food processor. Blend the ingredients continuously until you have the desired texture. If you prefer a coarser pesto, use the pulse setting instead. With the blender running, pour the olive oil in a steady thin stream to emulsify the oil with the ingredients. If needed, continue processing until the oil is combined with the ingredients. Taste the pesto and adjust the seasonings to your preference.

CHEF NOTES

Store the pesto in a small, airtight container or glass jar. You can also pour the pesto into ice cube trays and freeze. Remember to transfer the frozen pesto to a zip-lock bag once frozen. Homemade pesto can be stored in the refrigerator for up to 1 week.

Toasting the pine nuts really brings out their nutty sweetness. Heating the nuts releases their natural oils, intensifies their aroma and flavor, and makes them crunchier.

GRILLED LAMB OR CHICKEN PITA WRAPS

SERVINGS: 4 | PREP: 10 MINS | TOTAL: 25 MINS

INGREDIENTS

GRILLED LAMB OR CHICKEN KABOB

1-pound ground Lamb (or chicken if preferred)

1 teaspoon mustard

½ yellow onion, finely minced

2 cloves garlic, finely minced

1 teaspoon yellow curry powder

1 tablespoon ground cumin

½ teaspoon coarse salt

¼ teaspoon ground black pepper

TZATZIKI SAUCE

8 ounces plain Greek yogurt

2 cucumbers, small dice

1 tablespoon olive oil

juice of ½ lemon

1 tablespoon freshly chopped dill

3 cloves garlic, minced

lemon zest (optional)

salt & pepper, to taste

PITA BREAD FILLING

½ small red onion, sliced

1 tablespoon olive oil

4 pita breads, grilled

½ cup chopped romaine lettuce

1 Roma tomato, thinly sliced (optional)

½ cucumber, thinly sliced (optional)

½ cup feta cheese, crumbled

CHEF NOTES

This pita wrap can easily be changed into a platter or a bowl. I usually pair mine with quinoa or cauliflower rice. Both alternatives are healthier, and if you lose the pita, it makes the recipe gluten-free, and it lowers the carbohydrates, which helps if you are concerned about your carbohydrate intake.

DIRECTIONS

1. For the tzatziki sauce. Add all the tzatziki ingredients to a food processor and pulse until smooth. Taste and adjust the seasoning if necessary. Add the diced cucumber and fold in with a spatula. Spoon into a bowl and refrigerate. Alternatively, you can whisk all the ingredients together for a more textured sauce.

2. For the lamb or chicken kabobs. Combine all the ingredients in a bowl. Place in the refrigerator overnight to marinate (preferred) or for at least 1 hour. Preheat the grill to medium-high heat. Mold the meat in a log-shape around a wooden or metal skewer. Brush the meat with olive oil or spray with cooking spray. Place them on the grill and cook for 8-10 minutes, or until cooked through. Rotate the skewers a few times while grilling.

3. Grill the pita breads and then spread with tzatziki. Remove the meat from the skewer and slice into bite-size pieces. Pile the meat, tomatoes, romaine lettuce, cucumber and feta onto the pita.

NEXT

APPETIZERS & SNACKS

AT HOME WITH
Chef Mark Phillips

APPETIZERS & SNACKS

Dinner parties, entertaining, or just having friends over for drinks is something that I love to do. So, of course, food must be present when there are cocktails and wine. When it comes to catering, one of my favorite items to offer clients is "hors d'oeuvres" It's something about creating these beautiful bite-size appetizers that allow me to tap into my creative side. Whether the party is for 10 people or 600 the possibilities are endless.

Usually, when having a party or gathering there is some form of a theme or a reason; however, sometimes you just may want to have family and friends over just because. I wanted to share with you various dishes influenced by the cultures that inspire me. It is vital to streamline your time and preparation; therefore, you are not running around like a "chicken with its head cut off," no point intended (an old southern saying lol). Offering items that everyone can enjoy is key; some people have dietary restrictions such as gluten-free, nut-free, tomato allergies, etc. Most people eat with their eyes, so preparing visually appealing and tasty items is critical.

Any experienced host (or chef) will tell you that organization is the best approach for having a memorable party for you and your guest. Once you have narrowed down your menu, you want to give yourself enough time to shop and prep based on the time of the party and headcount (approximate as some people may or may not show up). Before going to the grocery store, make a note of ingredients not in your pantry, anything that needs special ordered, and tools that you may not have. Also, if you are serving cocktails, you can skip to the "It's 5oclock Somewhere" chapter and choose a signature drink(s) and make note of those ingredients.

Knowing how much to serve can be tricky sometimes.

If your gathering is family or friends, you usually have a good idea of how much they eat consistently; however, that is not always the case. Plan on two to three different offerings per guest, each is consuming two to three pieces of that item (on average). If the party extends into the dinner hour, I will offer items like dips, party wings, or antipasti, as these items will leave room for the main course.

For parties that may last all night or have no set end time, I would recommend appetizers and snacks that are easy to prepare in advance that do not require you to be in the kitchen throughout your event. You'll still have to do some last-minute work to bring everything together and take care of any recipes that must be made the same day they're being served.

There are no set-in-stone rules for putting together a menu for your gathering- the most important thing is to choose recipes that you and your guest will enjoy. Before you dive into the recipes, here is a recap of a few guidelines that can help you knock it out of the park: Stick to the theme, consider the setting, it's ok to keep it simple, pair with care, plan, make it ahead and appetizer for all. Grab yourself a beverage and put on your apron, but most of all, have fun; you can taste the love and passion in your food!

One of the first items I want to show you how to do is make a simple; charcuterie or crudité board. These boards most often consist of various vegetables, meats and cheeses and usually fruit or nuts, essentially a meat and cheese board! Perfect for grazing while guests arrive or just for you to nibble on while watching a movie or having a dialogue. Let's get creative!

CHARCUTERIE BOARDS

Charcuterie is the art of preparing cured or smoked meats. Putting together a charcuterie board is a snap which is why it is perfect for holiday parties, a friend gathering, or just because. Start by visiting the specialty department in your grocery store and pick and choose what looks fantastic and then set it on a board! Be sure to pile high with cured meats, cheeses, crackers, fruit, nuts, and more; this gorgeous and delicious spread will wow your guests. The remarkable thing about charcuterie boards is that there is no end to the possible variations. Switching up a few ingredients yields something new and unique each and every time. This is not exactly a recipe, but more a guide and list of ideas that might inspire you. Remember, you cannot go wrong!

MEATS

Prosciutto, salami, pepperoni, flavored turkey, ham, sausage, roast beef, lox (smoked salmon), pâtés, etc...

CHEESES

I LOVE cheese and aged hard cheeses like gouda, cheddar, and Manchego, but I also love soft cheeses like brie and gorgonzola. The board's beauty is that you can mix it up to fit everyone's taste! If you are unsure, ask the people behind the cheese counter at your local store! These days most popular grocery stores have a specialty cheese section.

FRUITS AND VEGGIES

Add fresh fruits like grapes, sliced apples, pears, berries, or melons. Dried mango, apricots, or dates can also be added to your platter. For the holidays: pomegranate seeds, fresh figs, and champagne grapes add a festive touch! Of course, all sliced veggies are welcome aboard, and adding an assortment of flavorful olives and pickles brings a nice salty element to the board.

BREAD AND CRACKERS

If you watch the carbs, you can skip these entirely and still have a fabulous board. But if you choose to include them, go for artisan bread and gourmet crackers with different shapes, textures, and flavors to keep things interesting! I love homemade toasted crostini or sliced French baguettes with olive oil drizzle.

DECORATING WITH GREENS

Add greens like kale leaves, basil, rosemary sprigs, or thyme to complete your board!

"Most of all, have fun creating your board as there is no wrong way!!!"

HONEY, SPREADS, OILS, AND VINEGAR

Set honey or honeycomb on the platter or place it in a small dish. Set out a plate of olive oil and balsamic vinegar for dipping bread! Dab, a generous amount of Adriatic fig or other fruit, spread on top of a log of goat cheese for spreading on bread and crackers.

NUTS AND SEEDS

Go big or go home; dried salted nuts are great, but I also encourage you to try Marcona almonds, spicy nut/seed mixes, caramelized nuts, and even chocolate-covered nuts or raisins.

SMOKED SALMON CREAM CHEESE & DILL CROSTINI

SERVINGS: 2 CUPS | PREP: 15 MINS | TOTAL: 20 MINS

INGREDIENTS

1 cup (8 oz) cream cheese

6 oz smoked salmon

¼ cup sour cream

1 tablespoon fresh lemon juice

¼ teaspoon cayenne pepper

¼ teaspoon smoked paprika

2 tablespoons capers, drained and rough chopped

2 tablespoon fresh dill, chopped

Chives, chopped (optional garnish)

Salt, to taste

DIRECTIONS

Combine the cream cheese, sour cream, mayonnaise, lemon juice, capers, and spices in a food processor fitted with a metal blade, and pulse until blended. Add the salmon and dill and pulse, scraping the sides of the bowl as necessary, until the salmon is finely chopped. Taste and add salt, if necessary. Serve as a dip with crackers, cucumbers (for a gluten-free option), and/or toasted crostini's.

CHEF NOTES

This dip can be made a couple of days in advance; however, it will become quite firm. Be sure to let sit out at room temperature at least an hour before serving; otherwise, the dip will be difficult to scoop.

PIMENTO CHEESE DEVILED EGGS

SERVINGS: 24 EGGS | PREP: 15 MINS | TOTAL: 30 MINS

INGREDIENTS

12 eggs

4 oz sharp cheddar

1/3 cup pimentos, diced and finely chopped

¼ teaspoon Tabasco

1 teaspoon yellow mustard

¼ teaspoon garlic powder

¼ teaspoon onion powder

salt & pepper to taste

Smoked paprika (garnish)

Chives (garnish)

DIRECTIONS

1. Bring a pot of water to boil with 2 teaspoons of salt. Place eggs in the pot and boil for 13-14 minutes. Remove from the hot water and place in a bowl of ice water or run under cold water for 5 minutes. Once cool, tap eggs on a hard surface, peel, and slice half lengthwise.

2. Remove yolks and place in the food processor (or bowl) with mayonnaise, tabasco, mustard, garlic, and onion powder. Gently fold in pimentos and cheese, season with salt and pepper to taste. Place in a piping bag, pipe filling into each egg, and sprinkle paprika and chives. Chill for at least one hour before serving.

PEACH & BURRATA BRUSCHETTA

SERVINGS: 8-10 PIECES | PREP: 10 MINS | TOTAL: 12 MINS

INGREDIENTS

1 teaspoon olive oil

1 French baguette or crusty Italian bread, sliced into 1" pieces

1 cup of burrata (1-2 ball of fresh burrata)

1 large peach, thinly sliced

1 teaspoon honey

6–7 large basil leaves, cut into ribbons

Cracked pepper

Prosciutto (optional)

Balsamic glaze (optional)

Salt to taste

DIRECTIONS

1. Pre-heat the oven to broil. Brush the slices of bread with a tiny bit of olive oil. (Spray olive oil works well here if you have it!) Toast the bread for 1-2 minutes until golden but not browned.

2. The burrata can be tricky to cut, but do not worry about making it perfect. Cut it in half, then slice each half into wedges. Spoon a slice of burrata onto each slice of bread and gently flatten with a spoon. Top each slice of bread with a slice of peach and then prosciutto.

3. Drizzle with honey, sprinkle basil, and a couple of turns of fresh cracked pepper. Add a sprinkle of salt. Add an optional drizzle of balsamic glaze.

CHEF NOTES

If you have never had burrata, you must try it. It's typically sold in the "gourmet" refrigerated cheese at the grocery store. You will generally find it in a container near fresh mozzarella. The outside of the burrata is made from mozzarella, and the inside is a combination of curds and cream. The interior is a bit like super creamy ricotta!

Although peaches are a summer fruit, you can also use this recipe for the spring, winter, or fall. Replacing the fruit with apples, pears, or using traditional Roma tomatoes.

BROWN SUGAR JERK GRILLED WINGS

SERVINGS: 6-8 | PREP: 15 MINS | TOTAL: 8 HOURS

INGREDIENTS

3 lbs chicken wings

2 tablespoons olive oil

4 tablespoons brown sugar

1/3 cup lime juice

2 tablespoons Worcestershire sauce

1 tablespoon garlic, minced

3-4 tablespoons jerk paste (Walkerswood or Grace)

CHEF NOTES

Preheat oven to 450 degrees. Line a baking sheet with aluminum foil and spray with cooking oil. Place wings on a baking sheet (reserve remaining marinade) bake for 25 minutes.

Brush the remaining marinade on the chicken and turn wings over. Bake for another 20 minutes. Take a thermometer and insert it into the bone; the temperature should read 165 degrees. Rest wings for 5 minutes before serving on a platter.

DIRECTIONS

1. In a large mixing bowl, whisk together jerk paste, olive oil, brown sugar, lime juice, Worcestershire, and garlic. Place chicken in a bowl with plastic wrap and marinate in the refrigerator for at least 8 hours or overnight (at minimum 4-6 hours).

2. Light a grill. Grill the chicken over a medium-hot fire, occasionally turning, until well browned and cooked through 35 to 40 minutes. (Cover the grill for a smokier flavor.) Transfer the chicken to a platter and serve.

HOMEMADE JERK SAUCE

1/4 cup allspice

1-3 scotch bonnet peppers

6 scallions, white and green parts, coarsely chopped

1/2 white onion, coarsely chopped

4 bay leaves, crumbled

1 tbs ginger, chopped or grated

1 cup fresh thyme leaves

1 tbs black pepper

2 tsp ground nutmeg

2 tsp ground cinnamon

Large dash kosher salt

juice from 1 lime

2 tablespoons Worcestershire sauce

1 cup vegetable oil

4 tablespoon brown sugar

KALE & CREMINI TURKEY MEATBALLS

SERVINGS: 4 | PREP: 20 MINS | TOTAL: 40 MINS

INGREDIENTS

THE MEATBALLS

1 lb. lean ground turkey

1/2 medium onion, grated

4-5 roasted garlic cloves, minced

1/4 cup finely chopped kale

1/4 cup finely chopped cremini mushrooms

1 Tbl fresh basil, chopped

1/2 tsp salt

2 tsp olive oil

1/2 tsp ground pepper

THE SAUCE

1 Tbl olive oil

1 small onion, chopped

3 roasted garlic cloves, minced

1 tsp ground oregano

2 Tbl chopped basil

1/4 tsp red pepper flakes

1/4 tsp salt

1/4 tsp ground pepper

1 (28 oz.) can crushed tomatoes

1 (14 oz.) can crushed tomatoes

6 basil leaves, thinly sliced

DIRECTIONS

1. Preheat the oven to 350 degrees F. In a large bowl, stir together the ground turkey, onion, garlic, basil, mushrooms, kale, salt, and pepper. Divide the mixture into 8 portions, form into balls, and set aside.

2. In a non-stick pan over medium-high heat and 2 tablespoons olive oil. Sear Meatballs on both sides (approximately 3 mins per side) and place on a plate, then set aside.

3. Use the same skillet from the meatballs. Heat the olive oil and set over medium heat. Add the onion and cook until softened, about 5 minutes. Stir in the garlic, oregano, red pepper flakes, bay leaves, salt, and pepper, and cook for 1 minute.

4. Add the crushed tomatoes, bring the sauce to a boil, and then simmer for 10-15 minutes. Stir in the basil. At this point, you can either leave the sauce as is or, if you would prefer a smooth sauce, place it in your blender for 1-2 minutes, then return it to pot. Nestle the meatballs into the sauce and spoon sauce over to coat the meatballs. Place in pre-heated oven and cook for 20 minutes. Remove from oven and let stand for 5-10 mins. Serve over pasta or rice, or on their own.

CHEF NOTES

If you want to use this same meatball recipe but without tomato sauce, you can replace its barbecue sauce. Follow steps 1-2 then take ½ cup brown sugar, ½ cup BBQ sauce, 2 tablespoon Worcestershire and 2 teaspoon chili flakes and add to the sauté pan. Bring to a simmer, add the meatballs, and cook for 10 minutes. Stirring occasionally.

CHICKEN OR BEEF SATAY

SERVINGS: 6-8 | PREP: 20 MINS | TOTAL: 1 HOUR 20 MINS

INGREDIENTS

16-20 bamboo skewers soaked in water

2 lbs beef, sirloin, cut into 1/4-inch thick, 3/4-1-inch cubes

Or

2 pounds boneless, skinless chicken thighs, cut into 1-inch chunks

1 tablespoon curry powder

2 teaspoons coriander

2-3 stalks lemongrass, white part only, cut into 1-inch length

1 teaspoon turmeric

3 cloves garlic, minced

1 tablespoon ginger, finely grated

1 tablespoon soy sauce

1 shallot, peeled, minced

1 tablespoon brown sugar

1 tablespoon lime juice

1 tablespoon canola oil

Salt & pepper to taste

FOR THE SAUCE

3 tablespoons natural creamy peanut butter

1 tablespoon reduced-sodium soy sauce

1 tablespoon fresh lime juice

2 teaspoon brown sugar

1 tablespoon garlic chili paste

1 teaspoon ginger powder

DIRECTIONS

1. To make the peanut sauce, whisk together peanut butter, soy sauce, lime juice, brown sugar, chili garlic sauce, and ginger in a small bowl. Whisk in 2-3 tablespoons water until desired consistency is reached; set aside.

2. In a medium bowl, combine lemongrass, soy sauce, curry powder, turmeric, garlic, ginger, brown sugar, coriander, and lime juice. In a gallon-size Ziploc bag or large bowl, combine chicken or beef and marinade mixture; marinate for at least 2 hours to overnight, turning the bag occasionally. Drain the chicken from the marinade, discarding the marinade,

3. Preheat grill to medium-high heat. Brush with canola oil; season with salt and pepper to taste. Thread chicken or beef onto skewers.

4. Add skewers to grill, and cook, occasionally turning, until the chicken is completely cooked through, reaching an internal temperature of 165 degrees F, about 12-15 minutes. For beef, depending on your personal internal temperature desire, you can cook medium-rare to 145 degrees or well done 165 degrees. Serve immediately with peanut sauce.

CRAB STUFFED MUSHROOMS

SERVINGS: 6-8 | PREP: 25 MINS | TOTAL: 40 MINS

INGREDIENTS

1 lb white mushrooms (or cremini for more flavor)

8 oz lump crabmeat

1 teaspoon Italian seasoning

1 tablespoon green onion, finely chopped

¼ cup red or green bell pepper (or both), minced

Ground black pepper to taste

¼ cup grated parmesan cheese

1/3 cup mayonnaise

3 tablespoons grated cheese

¼ teaspoon paprika

DIRECTIONS

1. Preheat the oven to 350 degrees. In a medium bowl combine crabmeat, green onions, Italian seasoning, and bell peppers. Mix in mayonnaise and ¼ cup parmesan cheese until well combined. Set aside in the refrigerator until ready to stuff mushrooms.

2. Wipe the mushrooms clean with a damp towel and remove the stems. You can scrape out the mushroom gills to make a deep pocket for stuffing. Fill the mushroom caps with a rounded teaspoon of filling and place on a lightly greased baking sheet, or you can use parchment paper with no grease. Sprinkle the tops with the parmesan and paprika.

3. Bake for 15 minutes, remove from the oven and serve immediately.

CHEF NOTES

You can replace the lump crab meat with claw meat; this is more cost-efficient; however you lose a little bit of quality.

BACON WRAPPED SHRIMP

SERVINGS: 15 | PREP: 15 MINS | TOTAL: 40 MINS

INGREDIENTS

1 teaspoons salt

1 teaspoon garlic powder

1 1/2 teaspoons paprika

1/2 teaspoon ground black pepper

1 teaspoon onion powder

1/2 teaspoon cayenne pepper

1 teaspoon dried oregano

1 teaspoon dried thyme

1/2 teaspoon red pepper flakes

2 tablespoons olive oil

1 tablespoon lemon juice

1 lb large shrimp, 16/20, peeled, deveined, tail on

12 ounces applewood bacon, 10 slices

1 tablespoon chopped parsley, for garnish

BBQ sauce (optional, dipping)

Sweet Chili (optional, dipping)

DIRECTIONS

1. Preheat oven to 400 degrees. Whisk together all spices, lemon juice, and olive oil in a medium-size bowl. Add shrimp and toss evenly, and allow to marinate for 20 -30 minutes while you prepare the bacon.

2. Cut bacon strips in half, about 4 to 5 inches in length. Line a baking sheet with foil or parchment, wrap one slice of bacon around one shrimp, and repeat with remaining bacon and shrimp until all are done.

3. Arrange the bacon-wrapped shrimp in a single layer on the baking sheet. Broil (or grill) for 8 minutes until bacon is crispy and sizzling. Flip and broil for another 2 minutes until shrimp are cooked through. Serve shrimp with your favorite dipping sauce!

CHICKEN TAQUITOS W/ CILANTRO LIME CREAM

SERVINGS: 6-8 | PREP: 15 MINS | TOTAL: 25 MINS

INGREDIENTS

3 cups chicken cooked and shredded

6 oz cream cheese softened (Optional)

1/3 cup sour cream

1/2 cup Mexican shredded cheese blend

1/4 cup green onion

1/4 cup chopped white onion

1/3 cup chopped red bell pepper

12 6 inch corn tortillas

vegetable or canola oil for frying

CILANTRO LIME CREAM

½ cup sour cream

1-2 tablespoon cilantro, finely chopped

¼ teaspoon garlic powder

¼ onion powder

Juice of half lime

DIRECTIONS

1. Heat half oil in a saucepan on medium heat. Cilantro lime cream - add all ingredients to a high-speed blender or food processor. Pulse until it is mostly smooth - you want to leave it slightly chunky with small, visible bits of cilantro.

2. In a large bowl mix together the chicken, cream cheese, sour cream, onion, shredded cheese, and peppers. Add salt and pepper to taste. Add a few tablespoons of chicken cheese mixture to the center of a tortilla and spread out. Repeat until all the tortillas are filled and rolled, set aside

3. Pour enough oil in a heavy bottom fry pan or pot to cover 1/2 inch, or so enough oil reaches halfway up the sides of the tortillas when frying. Heat the oil to 350°F — use a candy thermometer to measure the oil without touching the bottom of the pan. If you don't have a thermometer, test the oil temperature by dropping a piece of the tortilla into the oil. If it sizzles, it should be hot enough.

4. Add the filled tortillas to the hot oil and cook in batches so as not to crowd the pan. Fry each side until golden brown, about 2 minutes on each side. Transfer to a plate or cutting board lined with paper towels. Serve warm and ENJOY!

CHEF NOTES

Pre-heat oven to 425 degrees. Place seamed side down in a lightly greased 9×13 baking dish. Repeat with the remaining tortillas. Bake at 425 for 15 minutes. Serve immediately and enjoy!

SPINACH TORTELLINI & MOZZARELLA CAPRESE SKEWERS

SERVINGS: 18 SKEWERS | PREP: 10 MINS | TOTAL: 10 MINS

INGREDIENTS

2 packages spinach tortellini, cooked and cooled

2 pints cherry tomatoes

12 ounces fresh mozzarella, cubed

1/4 cup minced fresh basil

2 tablespoons pesto (see recipe)

1 tablespoon olive oil

Fig glaze (optional)

DIRECTIONS

1. In small bowl mix pesto and olive oil. On small skewers, thread 1 tortellini, 1 cherry tomato, and 1 mozzarella cube per skewer. Lay the skewers on a platter and lightly drizzle the dressing with a spoon.

2. Serve immediately or refrigerate. Sprinkle on the minced basil just before serving and fig glaze.

CRISPY GOAT CHEESE POPPERS WITH HOT HONEY

SERVINGS: 24 POPPERS | PREP: 10 MINS | TOTAL: 15 MINS

INGREDIENTS

1/3 cup all-purpose flour

½ teaspoon cracked pepper

1 large egg

½ teaspoon kosher salt

2/3 cup panko breadcrumbs

1 (11oz) log herb goat cheese (or plain)

2 cups canola or vegetable oil

2 tablespoons honey

¼ teaspoons cayenne pepper

¼ teaspoon chili flakes

2 tablespoons fresh chives chopped

DIRECTIONS

1. In a small bowl, mix honey, cayenne pepper, and chili flakes together and set aside. In a medium bowl, combine flour and black pepper. In a separate bowl, whisk together, egg, and 2 teaspoons water, and lastly in another bowl, add panko.

2. Roll goat cheese into 24 (1 tablespoon size) balls. Roll each ball in flour, then egg, and panko being sure to coat everything evenly. Repeat for each ball and freeze for 20-30 minutes, or until firm.

3. In a deep saucepan, heat oil on medium-high heat to 350 degrees (check the oil with a wooden spoon, if it sizzles oil is ready). Fry goat cheese balls in batches 1 to 2 minutes on each side until golden brown. Remove with a slotted spoon onto a paper towel. Arrange goat cheese poppers on a platter, drizzle with hot honey and garnish with chives.

CHEF NOTES

For baking- follow all the above steps until frying—Preheat oven to 450 degrees and line the baking sheet with parchment paper.

Place goat cheese balls on top of the parchment paper and spray with olive oil. Place in the center rack and bake for 8 minutes, however, check around the 6-minute mark to prevent burning. Remove with a slotted spatula and drizzle with hot honey and chives.

SHRIMP & GUACAMOLE WONTON CUPS

SERVINGS: 12 CUPS | PREP: 25 MINS | TOTAL: 40 MINS

INGREDIENTS

12 wonton wrappers

1 ½ tablespoon olive oil

Salt

FOR THE SHRIMP

2 teaspoons olive oil

12 large shrimp, peeled deveined, tail removed

1 lime

1 teaspoon chili powder

½ teaspoon smoked paprika

¼ teaspoon salt

¼ teaspoon black pepper

FOR GUACAMOLE

2 avocados

½ cup red onion, chopped

½ cilantro, finely chopped

½ cup Roma tomato, chopped

1 small jalapeno, small diced

1 lime

¼ cup sour cream

¼ teaspoon garlic powder

¼ tsp salt

DIRECTIONS

1. For guacamole – Scoop and cut avocados into small chunks. In a medium mixing bowl combine the avocado chunks with 1 tablespoon lime juice, salt, garlic powder, and sour cream, and mash with a potato masher or fork until you get a nice chunky texture.

2. Add tomatoes, red onions, cilantro, jalapeno peppers, and 1 more tablespoon of lime juice, stir and set aside in the refrigerator.

3. Wonton shells - Heat oven to 350 degrees F. Lightly brush wonton wrappers on both sides with olive oil. Lightly season one side with salt. Using a mini muffin pan, press the wonton wrappers down into the cups, lay back the corners, and press the bottoms down to make a defined cup. Bake until lightly browned, 8 to 10 minutes. Transfer to a rack and let cool.

4. Using a Microplane, zest the lime. Add the lime zest to the shrimp along with the olive oil, chili powder, salt, and pepper. Toss then arrange on a baking sheet in one layer. Bake until the shrimp are opaque throughout, 8 to 12 minutes. Set the lime aside for serving.

5. Fill the cup with about 1 tablespoon of guacamole and top with a shrimp. Garnish with a cilantro leaf.

CHEF NOTES

To make this entire appetizer dairy-free remove the sour cream from the guacamole. A few of the wonton cups may collapse during baking, making them difficult to stand up without falling over. We usually bake a few extras, just in case.

VEGETABLE SPRING ROLLS

SERVINGS: 24 SPRING ROLLS | PREP: 10 MINS | TOTAL: 30 MINS

INGREDIENTS

1 tablespoon coconut or olive oil

8 cups Napa cabbage, sliced thin (regular cabbage can be substituted)

2 cloves garlic, minced

½ cup edamame

2 carrots julienned (sliced thin)

¼ shiitake mushrooms, sliced thin

1 red bell pepper, sliced thin

2 ginger fresh, minced

¼ red onion, sliced thin

2 teaspoons sesame oil

2 tablespoons cornstarch

24 8" square spring roll wrappers

Canola oil for trying

Sweet Chili Sauce (for dipping)

DIRECTIONS

1. In a large sauté add 1 tablespoon of the cooking oil. Turn on the heat to medium-high and immediately add garlic, ginger, and red onion, stirring frequently. When the oil is hot, add the mushrooms, cabbage, peppers, carrots, and bamboo shoots.

2. In a small bowl, whisk together the cornstarch and 1/4 cup of cool water to form a slurry. Turn heat to high and stir-fry the vegetables for about 2 minutes and then toss in the edamame and sesame oil—Cook for another minute. Then spread the filling out onto a large baking sheet. Prop the baking sheet up on one side to allow any juices to accumulate at the bottom (and discard juices).

3. Place a spring roll wrapper on a flat surface, add 1-2 tablespoon of the vegetable mixture into a corner of the wrapper, and then roll the edge of the wrapper tightly around the mixture. Fold the two side corners towards the middle of the wrapper while continuing to roll up. Paint the top edge with the cornstarch slurry mixture and wrap tightly the rest of the way. Make sure all edges are tightly sealed. Place seam side down. Cover with plastic wrap to avoid drying out.

4. In a large wok or medium saucepan over high heat, add about 1-2 inches of cooking oil. Slide several egg rolls into the oil and allow them to cook for 2-3 minutes, turning them over a couple of times or until the wonton wrappers are golden brown. Remove the egg rolls to a cooling rack or paper-towel-covered plate to allow them to drain. Serve hot with sweet chili dipping sauce.

ROASTED RED PEPPER & GARLIC HUMMUS

SERVINGS: 4 | PREP: 10 MINS | TOTAL: 30 MINS

INGREDIENTS

¼ cup tahini

¼ cup fresh lemon juice (about 1 large lemon)

2 tablespoons extra virgin olive oil, plus more for serving

2 garlic cloves, minced

½ teaspoon ground cumin

1 teaspoon onion powder

½ teaspoon salt, or to taste

1 can (15 oz) chickpeas, drained & rinsed

¾ cup chopped roasted red bell peppers (bought-in jar of peppers)

CHEF NOTES

You can serve hummus with sliced cucumbers, a thick julienne of peppers and carrots or warm pita bread.

DIRECTIONS

1. To a food processor, add the tahini and lemon juice and process for 1 minute. Scrape the sides and bottom of the bowl with a spatula and process for a further 30 seconds. This extra processing time helps cream the tahini, which makes the hummus smooth and creamy.

2. Add the olive oil, minced garlic, cumin, onion powder and a ½ teaspoon of salt to the blended tahini and lemon juice. Process for 30 seconds and then scrape the sides and bottom of the bowl. Process for another 30 seconds, or until well blended.

3. Add half of the chickpeas to the food processor and process for 1 minute. Scrape sides and bottom of the bowl and then add the remaining chickpeas. Process until thick and quite smooth; 1 to 2 minutes.

4. Add the roasted peppers (reserve 1 tablespoon for later) and continue to process for a further 1 to 2 minutes, or until smooth. If the hummus is too thick or still has tiny bits of chickpea, then continue to process while slowly adding 1-3 tablespoons of water or olive oil until you have the desired consistency. Taste for salt and adjust if needed.

5. Finely chop the reserved tablespoon of peppers. Spoon the hummus into a bowl, make a small well in the middle and add the chopped peppers.

6. Store the homemade hummus in an airtight container and refrigerate up to one week.

ROASTED CORN SALAS

SERVINGS: 2-3 CUPS (EACH) | PREP: 20 MINS | TOTAL: 20 MINS

INGREDIENTS

3-4 ears corn, husks removed

1 jalapeno, split in half and deseeded

2 tablespoons olive oil

kosher salt and freshly cracked black pepper, to taste

2 firm Roma tomatoes, de seeded and diced

1 ripe avocado, diced

¼ small red onion, diced

3-4 tablespoons cilantro, finely chopped

juice of 2 limes

DIRECTIONS

1. Heat a grill to medium-high heat.

2. Add the corn and jalapeno to a sheet tray, drizzle with the olive oil and sprinkle with salt and pepper. Grill on all sides until lightly charre

SPINACH & ARTICHOKE DIP

SERVINGS: 6-8 | PREP: 10 MINS | TOTAL: 20 MINS

INGREDIENTS

1 8z oz package of cream cheese, room temperature

¼ cup mayonnaise

¼ cup asiago

¼ parmesan

2 garlic cloves, minced

¼ teaspoon onion powder

½ teaspoon Italian seasoning

¼ teaspoon kosher salt

1 14oz jar artichoke hearts, drained and chopped

½ - ¾ cup frozen or fresh (cooked) spinach, thawed and drained

¼ cup mozzarella shredded

Salt and pepper to taste

DIRECTIONS

1. Preheat the oven to 350 degrees. Lightly grease a small glass baking dish. In a medium bowl, mix cream cheese, mayonnaise, parmesan, asiago, garlic, salt, onion powder, Italian seasoning, and cracked pepper. Gently stir in the artichoke hearts and spinach.

2. Transfer the mixture to the prepared baking dish and top with mozzarella cheese. Bake in the pre-heated oven for 25 minutes until lightly browned and bubbly.

NEXT

COMING FROM WHERE I'M FROM

AT HOME WITH
Chef Mark Phillips

COMING FROM WHERE I'M FROM

I was born and raised in Winston-Salem, NC, which is where I had my first introduction to food. Family is my common association with food because growing up, no matter how far or near we gathered over food. I cannot think of any time frame where we did not eat and fellowship! My uncle Joe had a little farm in his backyard where he grew vegetables, raised chickens, and made biscuits from scratch. At his home, I was first introduced to the popular term "Farm-to-table." (Farm-to-table: food that has not been mass-produced, handled with care, and meant for quality and not quantity) I remember my mother reaping the harvest of my uncle's farm, whether from vast yield or because she needed to feed us due to financial hardship. In my uncle's mud room is where the canned vegetables were kept. Now I do not mean canned vegetables like the traditional associate you purchase from a grocery store; he did his canning. Canning is a method of preserving food in which the food contents are processed and sealed in an airtight container, a mansion jar. We would also be given some of those items, along with meats from his deep freezer. My mother's home seemed to be the "go-to" home for family gatherings. She (Gwen Hamlin) and my aunt Pat were the two who spearheaded the menu selection, which usually consisted of fried or baked chicken, macaroni and cheese, my mother's famous potato salad, collard greens, sweet potatoes, and more around holidays. My father's mother, Sylvia (my grandmother), is known for her stuffing and macaroni salad, which was and still is a must during Christmas. Whether I was with my mother's side of the family or my father's, there was always good food, drinks, laughs and sometimes crying. The takeaway that I apply in my adult relationships is family can be blood or chosen; however, unity amongst the people you love is what makes it special.

At times we had to be highly creative with meals! Some meals due to hardship may sound strange to some, for example, liver pudding sandwiches, smothered turkey necks and gravy, syrup sandwiches, or oodles of noodles. To be honest, I do not eat any of those items today; however, I learned that we made do with what we had. My mother also introduced me to my favorite seafood items: crab legs and calamari. I'll never forget when we were out to dinner with my uncle Jimmy, and they had ordered

influences exposed me to gumbo, pound cake, dirty rice, and oxtails, to name a few. The term "Soul Food" became popular in the 1960s with the Civil Rights Movement. As many blacks left the South to find better conditions and jobs in northern cities, they often had difficulty finding foods that were familiar to them. It's meant to remind them of home or food that feeds your soul. Growing up around these types of food has become quite second nature for me to prepare, and I do not need a recipe to follow because it has been ingrained in me. Do not fret. I have taken the time to write down some of my favorite recipes, but of course, with my own take, and I wanted to share them with you.

calamari; my mother said, "It's chicken, try it," and of course, being the curious kid, I ate it. The smiles and laughs had me second-guessing what I had eaten; after everyone composed themselves, she told me it was squid. It was too good for me to be disgusted, which made me consciously open to trying new foods.

Southern food can not only be restricted to what I grew up eating. Over the years and into high school, I began getting exposed to other southern foods. Technically the South also includes Florida, Louisiana, Texas, Georgia, and others. The term "Deep South" is usually applied to the first states that seceded before the U.S. Civil War and formed the Confederate States of America, which was below the Mason-Dixon Line. Those cultural

DIRECTIONS

1. **Biscuits** - Preheat oven to 425°F. Line a large baking sheet with parchment paper and set aside. In a large mixing bowl, whisk together the flour, baking powder, baking soda, sugar, rosemary, salt, and salt until well combined. Add in the cubed cold butter and cut into the dry ingredients using a fork or pastry cutter (you may also use a food processor for this step) until you have small pea-sized pieces of butter. Pour the cold buttermilk into the mixture and gently work it together until the dough starts to come together.

2. Scoop the dough onto a lightly floured surface and gently work it together with your hands. Pat the dough into a rectangle and fold it in thirds. Turn the dough, gather any crumbs, and flatten it back into a rectangle. Repeat this process two more times.

3. Place the dough onto a lightly floured surface and pat it down into a 1/2-inch thick rectangle (measure it if you need to). Using a floured 2.5-inch biscuit cutter, cut out the biscuits. Continue to gather any scrap pieces of dough, patting it back down to 1/2-inch thickness and cutting it until you have 12 biscuits. Arrange the biscuits on the baking sheet touching each other.

4. Bake at 425°F for about 15-17 minutes or until lightly golden brown. While the biscuits are in the oven, let's start the gravy; set a timer, so you do not forget about the biscuits.

5. **Gravy**- With your finger, tear small sausage pieces and add them in a single layer to a large, heavy skillet. Brown the sausage over medium-high heat until no longer pink. Reduce the heat to medium-low. Sprinkle on half the flour and stir so that the sausage soaks it all up, then add more little by little. Stir it around and cook it for another minute, then pour in the half and half, stirring constantly.

6. Cook the gravy, stirring frequently, until it thickens. (This may take a good 10 to 12 minutes.) Sprinkle in the onion powder, brown sugar, salt, and pepper, and continue cooking until very thick and luscious. If it gets too thick too soon, just add more half and half until desired thickness. Taste and adjust the seasoning.

7. Remove biscuits from the oven, let rest for 5-7 minutes and then cut biscuits in half (or leave them whole). Spoon the sausage gravy over warm biscuits and serve immediately!

INGREDIENTS

2 cups all-purpose flour

1 tablespoon baking powder

¼ teaspoons baking soda

2 teaspoons sugar

2-3 tablespoons fresh rosemary, finely chopped

2 tablespoons garlic, chopped

1 teaspoon salt

6 tablespoons cold unsalted butter, cubed

¾ cup cold buttermilk

GRAVY

1 lb breakfast sausage, pork, or chicken

1/3 cups all-purpose flour

3 ½ cups half and half, more to taste

½ teaspoon brown sugar

½ teaspoon onion powder

½ teaspoon salt

½ teaspoon freshly ground black pepper, more to taste

ROSEMARY GARLIC BISCUITS & GRAVY

SERVINGS: 12 | PREP: 15 MINS | TOTAL: 30 MINS

CHEF NOTES   If trying to cook the biscuits and gravy simultaneously is intimidating, you can do each step separately. Also, if you like more of a peppered gravy up your black pepper quantity to 1 ½ teaspoon or add your own to your plate.

FRIED GREEN TOMATOES & REMOULADE SAUCE

SERVINGS: 6 | PREP: 5 MINS | TOTAL: 20 MINS

INGREDIENTS

3-4 large green tomatoes, firm

2 eggs

½ cup milk

1 tablespoon Cajun seasoning

½ cup cornmeal

1 cup all-purpose flour

½ cup panko breadcrumbs

Vegetable oil

REMOULADE SAUCE

¾ cup mayonnaise

1 tablespoon Dijon mustard

¼ teaspoon Texas Pete (or your favorite hot sauce)

1 teaspoon lemon juice

2 teaspoon garlic powder

2 teaspoons Cajun seasoning

GARNISH

Crumbled goat cheese

Green onions, sliced thin

DIRECTIONS

1. Remoulade Sauce - Combine ingredients in a bowl. Set aside, covered, in the refrigerator.

2. In a heavy bottom pan, pre-heat oil to 350 degrees. Season tomatoes, on both sides, with Cajun seasoning. Place flour in a shallow dish. In another shallow dish, beat eggs with the milk. In another container, mix panko breadcrumbs and garlic powder. Dredge tomatoes through the flour, then the eggs, and then through the breadcrumbs. Add only a few pieces to the fryer at a time so that they can cook evenly for about 2 to 3 minutes.

3. Drain tomatoes on a paper towel, on a plate, place tomatoes however you desire, and drizzle some of the remoulade sauce, then goat cheese and green onions.

BLACKENED SHRIMP & GRITS

SERVINGS: 4 | PREP: 10 MINS | TOTAL: 30 MINS

INGREDIENTS

1 lb shrimp, 21-25, peeled and deveined

1 tablespoon garlic, minced

½ cup red and green bell peppers, small diced

½ cup yellow onion, small diced

1 teaspoon fresh thyme

3 tablespoons olive oil

1 cup heavy cream

BLACKENED SEASONING

2 tablespoons smoked paprika

1 teaspoon cayenne pepper

½ teaspoon black pepper

1 tablespoon dried thyme

1 tablespoon garlic powder

1 tablespoon onion powder

1 ½ teaspoon kosher salt

FOR THE GRITS

1 cup quick grits

2 cups of water

1 cup heavy cream

4 tablespoons unsalted butter

½ teaspoon garlic powder

½ teaspoon onion powder

¼ teaspoon salt

¼ teaspoon black pepper

DIRECTIONS

1. In a large saucepan, bring water, salt, pepper, onion, and garlic powder to a boil. Slowly stir in grits. Stir and pour gradually, so you don't get any lumps. Reduce heat to medium-low; cook, covered, until thickened; after about 5 minutes, slowly add in heavy cream, stirring occasionally. Remove from heat. Stir in butter until melted; keep warm.

2. In a small bowl, mix all the ingredients for the blackened seasoning. In a medium-sized bowl add your shrimp and take about 2 tablespoons of the blackened seasoning, coat evenly. Meanwhile, in a large skillet over medium-high heat, add shrimp and sauté for 2-3 minutes on each side; remove shrimp from the pan.

3. Add remaining olive oil, peppers, onion, and thyme. Cook for 2 to 3 minutes, add garlic, sauté for 1 minute, and then add heavy cream. Bring to a simmer and reduce heat, cook for approximately 5-7 mins for the sauce to reduce, and add in shrimp. Remove from heat and let stand. Divide grits among 4 serving bowls: top with blackened shrimp and cream sauce. Garnish with chopped parsley.

BAKED MACARONI & CHEESE

SERVINGS: 8-10 | PREP: 20 MINS | TOTAL: 40 MINS

INGREDIENTS

1 lb dried elbow pasta

½ cup salted butter (1 stick)

4 whole eggs

1 cup whole milk

1 cup heavy cream

2 cups grated medium cheddar cheese

1 cup grated sharp cheddar cheese

1 cup grated mozzarella

1 cup Colby jack cheese

1 cup parmesan cheese

½ tablespoon salt

1 teaspoon black pepper

2 teaspoon garlic powder

2 teaspoons onion powder

DIRECTIONS

1. Heat the oven to 375 degrees. Rub a 9x13 inch baking dish with a little butter.

Bring a large amount of water to boil in a large pot.

2. Add the pasta and a generous amount of salt. Cook until the pasta is al dente, then drain and set aside. In that same pot, add butter, heavy cream, and milk, heat for 5 mins on medium just until butter is melted, and remove from heat. Whisk in salt, black pepper, onion powder, garlic powder, and eggs. You want to temper the eggs; therefore, they do not scramble.

3. In a large bowl, mix together all your cheese, reserve 1 ½ cup of cheese, and set aside. Add half of your drained noodles to the pot and half of the cheese and stir, then add the remaining noodles and cheese. Transfer the mixture to your buttered baking dish and top with reserved cheese.

4. Bake in the oven for 30 minutes until bubbly and golden. If the pasta becomes bubbly before the top is golden, you can turn your oven on broil for a minute or two to crisp the topping. Let stand for 10 minutes and serve.

JALAPENO CHEDDAR CORN BREAD

SERVINGS: 8-10 | PREP: 10 MINS | TOTAL: 40 MINS

INGREDIENTS

1 ½ cup yellow cornmeal

1 cup all-purpose flour

3 tsp baking powder

1 tsp kosher salt

1 tablespoon sugar

2-3 jalapeno peppers, finely chopped (depending on your spice level)

1 cup sharp cheddar cheese, shredded

¾ cup Vermont white cheddar, shredded

1 cup fresh corn kernels

1 ¼ cup buttermilk

1/3 cup butter, melted

2 large eggs

DIRECTIONS

1. Preheat oven to 400 degrees. Grease and lightly coat a 9-inch baking dish with flour and set aside. In a large mixing bowl, combine the cornmeal, flour, baking powder, sugar, and salt; whisk together until thoroughly combined. Add the grated cheese and chopped jalapeno, then fold in the freshly shucked corn kernels.

2. In a separate bowl, whisk together buttermilk, melted butter, and eggs. Pour over reserved dry ingredients and stir delicately with a spoon until just combined. Grab your prepared baking dish and pour your cornbread mixture into the pan.

3. Bake for 25 minutes or until the top is golden brown. To check doneness, take a toothpick and insert it into the center; if it comes out clean, it is done. Allow to cool for a few minutes, cut into 8-10 pieces, and serve with butter.

CHEF NOTES

I prefer to put a little extra butter on the cornbread as soon as it comes out of the oven. If this is something you would like to do, take about 1-2 tablespoons of butter on a fork or spoon and gently run it along the top of the cornbread, as watch it slowly melt from the heat.

DIRECTIONS

1. In a large mixing bowl, place, your chicken wings. In a small bowl, combine salt, paprika, black pepper, garlic powder, onion powder, dried thyme, and cayenne pepper. Take half of the seasoning mixture, toss the chicken, and set aside.

2. Add flour, cornstarch, and remaining seasoning to a plastic bag, zip closes the bag, and shake well. In another bowl, whisk together egg whites and hot sauce. Dip chicken pieces in hot sauce egg mixture, a few at a time, put them in the bag with the flour, seal the bag and shake to coat well. Place the coated chicken on a cookie sheet or tray, set aside at room temperature for at least 10 minutes while you set up for frying, and heat the oil.

3. Place the oil in a large Dutch oven, attach a candy or deep-fry thermometer, and heat over medium-high heat until the oil is 350°F, about 15 minutes. If you do not have a deep-fry thermometer, you can take a wooden spoon or flour and test to see if the oil sizzles when it comes in contact.

4. Using tongs, place 3-6 pieces of the chicken (depending on the size) in the oil and fry, using tongs to rotate the pieces every 3 to 4 minutes and adjusting the heat as needed to maintain 325°F, until golden-brown with an internal temperature of 165°F (check by inserting a probe thermometer into the thickest part of the chicken without touching bone), 12 to 15 minutes. Immediate dust the hot chicken with ranch seasoning. Transfer the chicken to the rack on the second baking sheet or plate with a paper towel. Make sure the oil comes back up to 350°F before frying the remaining chicken in 2 more batches. Let cool at least 10 minutes before serving.

DUSTED RANCH FRIED CHICKEN WINGS

SERVINGS: 6-8 | PREP: 15 MINS | TOTAL: 45 MINS

INGREDIENTS

1 lb chicken wings, rinse, and pat dry

2 tablespoons kosher salt

2 tablespoons smoked paprika

1 ½ tablespoon black pepper

2 tablespoon garlic powder

2 tablespoon onion powder

2 teaspoon dried thyme

2 teaspoons cayenne pepper

2 cups all-purpose flour

2 tablespoons cornstarch

3 tablespoons hot sauce

2 large egg whites, fresh

3 quarts vegetable or peanut oil, for deep frying

1 pack of buttermilk hidden valley ranch seasoning

CHEF NOTES

A southern tradition is using a cast iron pan to fry the chicken in; however, if you are not experienced in frying in a semi-shallow pan, I recommend a deep Dutch oven-style pot. The Dutch oven's high sides will reduce the amount of oil that splatters out of the pan, but you can also minimize splashing by using long tongs to lower your chicken into the hot oil.

Use another pair of tongs to remove the chicken from the oil, holding the finished chicken over the hot oil for 10 to 15 seconds so excess oil can drip back into the Dutch oven and not all over your stovetop.

You may also want a plate, small baking sheet, or foil to rest oily tongs or equipment while frying.

NEW ORLEANS INSPIRED GUMBO

SERVINGS: 8 | PREP: 30 MINS | TOTAL: 1 HOUR 40 MINS

INGREDIENTS

¼ cup canola oil

1 lb chicken thigh, boneless and skinless (or breast)

6-8 oz smoked sausage (pork or chicken)

3-4 tablespoons olive oil

½ cup flour

1 medium onion diced

2 teaspoons minced garlic

1 medium green bell pepper diced

1 cup chopped celery

½ cup lump crab (or crab legs)

1 tablespoon Cajun seasoning

1 tablespoon thyme fresh

2 bay leaves

6-7 cups chicken stock (sub with water)

1 lb shrimp, peeled and deveined

1 tablespoon gumbo file

2 green onions, chopped (optional garnish)

¼ cup chopped parsley (optional garnish)

Cooked rice

CHEF NOTES

Gumbo is a soup famous in the U.S. state of Louisiana and is the official state cuisine. Gumbo consists primarily of a strongly-flavored stock, meat or shellfish, a thickener, and what Louisianians call the "Holy Trinity" of vegetables, namely celery, bell peppers, and onions.

Adjust the thickness of the soup and flavor with broth or water and salt. The key to this recipe is the roux, A "roux" is made with two ingredients: flour and oil, and it's the key to any excellent gumbo recipe! The flour and oil are cooked and stirred together for about 20-30 minutes until it becomes dark brown, almost like mud or chocolate, and the consistency of dough. The roux is what adds the deep, rich flavor to the gumbo, and it gives it its thick texture.

DIRECTIONS

1. Lightly season the chicken with salt and pepper. Heat the oil over medium heat in a heavy-bottomed pot; the chicken until browned on both sides and remove. Add the sausage and cook until browned, and then remove. Set aside. In a large Dutch oven or heavy-bottomed saucepan, combine olive oil and flour until smooth.

2. Cook on medium heat, stirring continuously, for about 20- 30 minutes or until it turns a rich medium-dark brown color. (Side Note: Do not walk away from the stove during this process. It might burn.) Remove from stove and let it cool. Return the Dutch oven back to the stove. Add the onion, garlic, green pepper, and celery and cook for 8- 10 minutes –stirring frequently.

3. Then add gumbo file, chicken, sausage, Cajun seasoning, thyme, and bay leaves, and let it cook for 5 minutes. Add chicken stock a little at a time until evenly incorporated. Bring to a boil and let it simmer for about 45 – 50 minutes. Add the crab and shrimp, and simmer for 7-10 more minutes. Garnish with green onions and chopped parsley.

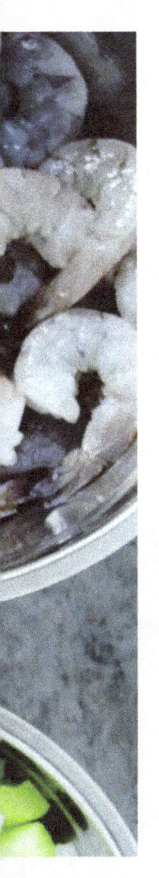

MY "MOMMA'S" POTATO SALAD

SERVINGS: 10 | PREP: 10 MINS | TOTAL: 40 MINS

INGREDIENTS

- 4-5 medium potatoes, peeled and cubed
- 5 boiled eggs
- ½ yellow onion, chopped
- ¼ cup dill pickle, small diced
- ¾ cup mayonnaise (I prefer Dukes)
- 2 tablespoons yellow mustard
- ½ teaspoon salt
- ½ teaspoon place pepper
- ½ garlic powder
- ½ teaspoon white sugar
- 2 teaspoon white vinegar
- 1 teaspoon pickle juice
- Smoked paprika or cayenne pepper (optional garnish)

DIRECTIONS

1. Bring a large pot of water to boil over high heat. When the water starts to boil, add 2 teaspoons of kosher salt and the potato cubes and cook for approximately 10 minutes. The potatoes are cooked when you can take a piece of potato and mash it with a fork with little resistance. Drain the potatoes in a colander.

2. Pour the drained and cooked potatoes back into the pan and use a potato masher to mash them 2-3 times, be careful not to mash too much as you want some texture. This step makes your potato salad even creamier and ensures that the potatoes soak up more of the mayonnaise mixture.

3. While the potatoes are cooking, combine the mayonnaise, mustard, onion, pickles, vinegar, pickle juice, hard-boiled eggs, garlic powder, sugar, salt, and pepper in a large bowl and mix well. Add the cooked potatoes and fold in. Taste and adjust with salt and pepper. Garnish with a dash of paprika. Refrigerate and serve chilled. Enjoy!

SOUTHERN COLLARD GREEN

SERVINGS: 8 | PREP: 15 MINS | TOTAL: 1 HOUR 10 MINUTES

INGREDIENTS

2 lbs fresh collards, wash and chopped

1 lb smoked turkey (necks, wings, or legs)

1 large onion, chopped

3 cloves garlic, minced

1 teaspoon chili flakes

1 teaspoon black pepper

2 teaspoon salt

2 teaspoon apple cider vinegar

2 teaspoons hot sauce

3 quarts chicken stock

DIRECTIONS

1. Place smoked turkey, onion, garlic, chili flakes, black pepper, salt, hot sauce, and vinegar in a large stockpot with the chicken stock. Bring to a boil, reduce heat to simmer, and let cook for at least 30 minutes. At this point take a spoon and taste the beginning stage of your "pot liquor." At this point, this is the essence that your greens will take on.

2. Stir collard greens into the pot and bring to a boil. Reduce heat to simmer, and cook for 30 minutes, or until greens are tender—season with additional salt and pepper to taste. I like mine with a little spice, so I add a few more dashes of hot sauce.

CHEF NOTES

To make your greens completely vegan, remove the smoked turkey from the recipe, and follow the remaining steps. If you want a smoky flavor, you can opt to use liquid smoke; however, the taste is very dominating, so you do not need a lot. You would add the liquid smoke at the beginning of this recipe.

Pot Liquor- Liquid from boiling greens (collard greens, mustard greens, turnip greens); sometimes salt, smoked pork, or smoked turkey.

NOT-SO TRADITIONAL "CHICKEN POT PIE"

SERVINGS: 8 | PREP: 20 MINS | TOTAL: 50 MINS

INGREDIENTS

2 tablespoons unsalted butter

2 tablespoons olive oil

1 lb. boneless skinless chicken breast, cut into small bite-size pieces

½ cup carrots, sliced

½ cup baby portabella mushrooms, sliced

1/2 cup yellow onion, chopped

1 ¼ teaspoons salt

1 teaspoon garlic, chopped

½ teaspoon dried thyme leaves

¼ teaspoon ground black pepper

¼ cup all-purpose flour

½ cup heavy cream

1 cup chicken broth

¼ cup fresh parmesan cheese, grated (optional)

1/2 cup broccoli florets, small copped

2 unbaked pie crusts (could use pre-made refrigerated - 1 box)

DIRECTIONS

1. Preheat oven to 425 degrees F. Make sure there is an oven rack on the bottom rack of the oven. Add the butter and olive oil to a large skillet over medium heat. Once the butter is melted, add the chicken, carrots, mushrooms, onion, salt, garlic, thyme leaves, and pepper. Cook for 8-10 minutes, until the chicken, is cooked, stirring often.

2. Add the flour. Stir well until no dry flour remains. Slowly stir in the cream, then the chicken broth. Cook until bubbling and thick; add parmesan cheese, often stirring 3-4 minutes.

3. Remove from the heat. Stir in the broccoli. Let this cool for 15 minutes before filling the pie. Fit one pie crust into a 9-inch pie plate. Spoon in semi-cooled filling into the pie crust. Top with the second pie crust. Seal the edges of the pie crust together with your fingers or fork. Cut 3-4 slits in the top crust to allow steam to escape.

4. Place the filled pie plate on a baking sheet. Bake for 30 minutes on the bottom rack of the oven. Cool for 15-30 minutes before slicing and serving.

BBQ PORK SPARERIBS

SERVINGS: 6 | PREP: 10 MINS | TOTAL: 4 HOURS

INGREDIENTS

2 racks, Spareribs, membrane removed

DRY RUB

2 tablespoons kosher salt

1 tablespoon paprika

1 teaspoon cumin

2 teaspoons ground mustard

1 teaspoon cayenne pepper

½ teaspoon black pepper

2 teaspoon onion powder

2 teaspoon garlic powder

BBQ SAUCE

1 tablespoon olive oil

1 tablespoon onion powder

2 clove garlic, minced

½ teaspoon ground cumin

½ cup ketchup

1 tablespoon sriracha

1 tablespoon Worcestershire

2 tablespoon brown sugar

2 teaspoon Dijon mustard

1 tablespoon apple cider vinegar

Salt and pepper taste

DIRECTIONS

1. Preheat oven to 275-300 degrees. Combine all the ingredients for the dry rub in a small bowl. Place each rack of ribs on a double layer of foil; sprinkle rub all over ribs. Wrap racks individually and divide between 2 baking sheets.

2. Cover the pan or baking sheet tightly with aluminum foil, and then bake until the meat falls easily from the bones, 3 to 4 hours.

3. While the ribs bake, make the barbecue sauce. Heat the olive oil in a saucepan over medium heat. Add the garlic and cook until soft and translucent, 3 to 5 minutes. Stir in onion powder, and cumin and cook for an additional 30 seconds.

4. Add the ketchup, sriracha sauce, brown sugar, Worcestershire, and apple cider vinegar. Stir to combine, season with salt, then cook for 2 minutes. Set aside in preparation for the ribs to finish roasting.

5. Carefully open each packet and drain the drippings into a saucepan. You may only need the drippings from one packet. Set ribs aside. Simmer the drippings over medium-high heat until the sauce thickens, about 5 minutes.

6. Slather the baked ribs with barbecue sauce, then broil the ribs for 5 to 7 minutes until the sauce is caramelized.

CHEF NOTES

For a grilled taste! Skip step six and start here, build a medium-hot fire in a charcoal grill, or heat a gas grill to high. Grill ribs, basting with barbecue sauce mixture and frequently turning, until lacquered and charred in places and heated through 7-10 minutes. Transfer to a cutting board; cut between ribs to separate. Transfer to a platter and serve with additional barbecue sauce.

GEORGIA PEACH COBBLER

SERVINGS: 10 | PREP: 20 MINS | TOTAL: 40 MINS

INGREDIENTS

½ cup unsalted butter

1 cup all-purpose flour

1 ½ cup sugar

½ cup brown sugar

2 teaspoons baking powder

¼ teaspoon salt

1 cup milk

4-6 fresh peaches, sliced

2 teaspoon corn starch

1 ½ teaspoon cinnamon

½ teaspoon allspice

2 teaspoon lemon juice

DIRECTIONS

1. Preheat oven to 375 degrees. Melt butter in a 13- x 9-inch baking dish.

2. Combine flour, 1 cup sugar, baking powder, and salt; add milk, stirring just until dry ingredients are moistened. Pour batter over butter (do not stir).

3. Take the remaining 1 cup sugar, brown sugar, peach slices, cinnamon, allspice, cornstarch, and lemon juice to a boil over high heat, stirring constantly; pour over batter (do not stir). Sprinkle with cinnamon, if desired.

4. Bake 35-45 minutes at 350°F until the batter comes to the top and is golden brown. Serve warm with ice cream.

BANANA PUDDING

SERVINGS: 12 | PREP: 20 MINS | TOTAL: 3 HOURS 20 MINS

INGREDIENTS

1 package instant vanilla pudding mix

2 cups cold milk

1 can sweeten condensed milk

1 teaspoon vanilla extract

2 cups heavy cream

1 block cream cheese, room temperature

4 bananas, sliced

1 box vanilla wafers (chessman or shortbread cookies)

DIRECTIONS

1. In a large mixing bowl, combine milk, vanilla pudding mix, and sweetened condensed milk. Whisk thoroughly, breaking up any lumps, and refrigerate for at least 5 minutes or until set.

2. In another large bowl, combine heavy cream and vanilla. Beat until stiff peaks form, 2 to 3 minutes. Set aside half of the mixture for topping the dish. Fold the remaining half into the pudding mixture. Line the bottom of a 13x9 baking dish with one package of cookies of your choosing. Top with sliced bananas.

3. Top with one-third of the pudding mixture. Cover with another layer of wafer cookies. Continue layering the pudding, wafer cookies, and banana slices until you reach the top, ending with a final layer of banana pudding.

4. Top with the remaining package of cookies. Cover with plastic wrap and refrigerate for 4 hours.

CHEF NOTES

Store airtight for up to 3 days. You can make this pudding up to 48 hours in advance. Any longer and the bananas will begin losing moisture, so it's best to stick to 2 days or less. I do not recommend freezing this due to the delicate ingredients. The pudding will get a little mushy and thin out as it thaws. French Vanilla or Banana Pudding Mix can be substituted for the vanilla flavor.

BRAISED OXTAILS

SERVINGS: 4-6 | PREP: 15 MINS | TOTAL: 4 HOURS, 10 MINS

INGREDIENTS

2 –3 tablespoon cooking oil

1– 2 lbs oxtail cut up medium pieces

4-5 tablespoons Graces Oxtail & Stew Seasoning

1 yellow onion chopped

1 tablespoon garlic, smashed

2 teaspoons ginger, minced

3-4 springs fresh thyme

1/2 teaspoon allspice

1-2 teaspoon curry powder

1/2 cup baby carrots

1 tablespoon ketchup

1 Whole Scotch bonnet pepper

2 green onions chopped

1 Tablespoon Worcestershire sauce

2-3 cups vegetable or beef stock

2 cups water

15 ounce can butter beans, rinsed and drained (optional)

Salt to taste

CHEF NOTES

DIRECTIONS

1. Season oxtail with graces oxtail seasoning. Set aside. I recommend at least marinating the meat for 8 hours or let sit overnight for full flavor impact.

2. In a large pot, heat oil over medium heat until hot, and add the oxtails to the pot, working in batches, then allowing them to cook, occasionally turning until they are well browned. Remove oxtails to a bowl and keep warm. Add half of the onions, garlic, and ginger to the pot, along with the pepper, curry powder, thyme, allspice, and a third of the scallions, and stir to combine. Allow to cook until softened, approximately 5 minutes.

3. Return the oxtails to the pot along with any accumulated juices and put water and stock into the pot so that the oxtails are almost submerged. Bring to a simmer and then cook, covered, for approximately 1 hour, stirring occasionally.

4. Add remaining onions, garlic, and ginger to the pot and another third of the scallion, carrots, and Worcestershire sauce. Stir to combine and continue to cook until the meat is yielding and loose on the bone, approximately one hour longer. Remove approximately one cup of liquid from the pot and place it in a small bowl. Add flour to this liquid and stir to combine, working out any lumps with the back of a spoon. Add this slurry to the pot along with ketchup, then stir to combine and allow to cook a further 15 minutes or so. Remove Scotch bonnet pepper and thyme stems. Fold butter beans into the stew and allow these to heat through. Scatter remaining scallions over the top. Serve with white rice or rice and peas.

This recipe was inspired by my bonus Jamaican grandmother Sonia Charles. Although some may not consider south Florida part of the South, however, it is the southernmost state.

NEXT

WHAT IS FOR DINNER?

AT HOME WITH
Chef Mark Phillips

WHAT IS FOR DINNER?

I am sure that at some point in our everyday lives, we find ourselves saying, "What's for Dinner?" Single, married or having dinner with friends; it does not make matter because we all must eat. Too often, people ask me what my specialty is, and most people are looking for the answer to be a type of dish, genre, style, or method. Honestly, my specialty is bringing people together over food that I love to create. The origin and method are among the many layers that add to the culinary experience.

Growing up, I recognized food's potential to deepen the conversation, build relationships, and increase laughter.

Holidays usually are when the number of people gathered exceeds my immediate household. We would have a few tables spread throughout whomever home dinner was taking place, and of course, there was the "kids" table. Since my family is from the south, most of our dinners started with a prayer, setting the tone by giving thanks for everyone fellowshipping together. Family and dinner go hand and hand for me, so rightfully so; having that foundation fueled me into wanting to have that own dynamic in my own adult life.

College was where I began to start my own tradition of gathering over dinner. I studied culinary arts in college, so of course, there were several of my friends who could cook, and we would find ourselves getting together to eat and drink.

We were not your typical college students; there were no microwave dinners and drive-thru fast food; we were cooking! Chef Max & Chef Turbo were my cooking partners at that time; no matter where we were, it would be at least one of us cooking, if not in some form or fashion, all of us cooking. Backyard barbecue, football, finger foods, or special occasion dinners, no moment to commune was left unturned. Give us a good libation, friends, and food; we were sure to have a good time with long-lasting memories.

Later in my adult life, a few years after I arrived in Atlanta, GA, I started to build my own bonus family where I would host friends and family in my home. I would have people over, and we would eat, and I would introduce the "Conversation bowl" guest would choose a topic or question from the bowl, and we would discuss it after dinner. Mama Jaaz coined the "Love Circle," and she hosts people in her home where we would love on and support one another. We were in piedmont park one day celebrating Easter, and I said, "I feel like cooking,"? and she said, "I have a kitchen." From that day on, no matter how near or far, we spread love and light over food and conversation. Dining together can radically shift people's perspectives: It can reduce people's perceptions of inequality, and diners tend to view those of different races, genders, and socioeconomic backgrounds as more equal than they would in other social scenarios.

I love to curate dinner menus for clients, well hell, even friends for that matter. If there is no theme, I usually ask what some are likes or dislikes, allergies, and/or preferences. From there, I go on a mental journey, building layers in my mind of ingredients that pair well together or complement one another. There are so many foods that I have adopted into my style of cooking, which I like to call "American Fusion." Within these recipes, I'm going to take you on an expedition where you can share with the ones you love or simply try something new for yourself.

I briefly covered some of the cooking methods at the beginning of this book when I reintroduced you to your kitchen however I wanted to go into a little more description of 12 methods. Several of these methods I refer to in the recipe and others will help you with cooking in general.

SAUTÉING is probably the most common method everyone uses daily, assuming you cook LOL. The French word Sauter means "to jump." Sautéed food is cooked and stirred in a small amount of fat or oil over moderately high heat in an open, shallow pan. Before you start sautéing, ensure your food is cut into same-size pieces—otherwise, it will cook unevenly. You can sauté just about anything, including ground meats, chicken breasts, and veggies.

GRILLING is most associated with the spring and summer seasons; however, it can be done any time of the year. Nowadays, with modern technology, you don't necessarily need an open flame to create the effects of a grill; however, you sacrifice the flavor and essence of smoke. The two most common style of grilling is either over charcoal or wood and gas. Some would argue that one tastes better than the other, but like most things, each has its pros and cons. With gas, you can better control the heat and have an instant flame, whereas with charcoal or wood, you have to gauge your heat to the best of your ability unless you have a thermometer. Then you go into direct or indirect heat. For direct grilling, food is placed on the grill directly over the heat source and can be cooked, covered, or uncovered. Generally, direct grilling is best for foods that cook quickly because they're tender, petite, or thin (think burgers, hot dogs, and veggies). Indirect grilling means placing the food adjacent to the heat source and covering the grill so the hot air circulates. This allows for cooking the food from all sides and eliminating the need for flipping. Indirect grilling is best suited for larger foods that take longer to cook, like ribs and whole birds.

PAN-FRYING can be easily confused with sautéing; however, pan-frying involves cooking foods that may have a light breading or coating in a skillet with a small amount of hot oil or fat. Thin cuts of meat or fish work best with this method as the surface of the food browns and will become crispy if coated. Pan-frying is not the same as **deep frying**, as deep frying involves complete submersion of the item that is being fried.

STIR-FRYING is a method that is most associated with Asian culture. To stir-fry is to quickly cook small, uniform pieces of food in a little hot oil over medium-high heat. Foods need to be stirred constantly to prevent burning. You do not need to invest in a fancy wok (although I prefer to stir-fry in a wok); a large skillet will work fine.

SEARING means browning a food, usually meat, on all sides using high heat. Searing is a quick-cooking method that generally involves finishing your meat or roast using another technique. The purpose of searing is mainly for color and to increase the flavor of whatever seasoning and spices you have put onto the protein.

To **Broil** means cooking food a measured distance below direct, dry heat. Broiling is a great way to give your food a crispy, crunchy outer layer. It's best to position the oven rack while the oven is cold so you do not get burned. Position the pan and its rack, so the surface of the food (not the rack) is the specified distance from the heat source; you could end up accidentally over-or undercooking your food.

Turkeys and thanksgiving are when most people think of **Roasting**. Roasting is when you cook food with dry heat, uncovered, in a large oven. Large items, like poultry or roast beef, are usually placed in a roasting pan to allow the melted fat to drip away. Not to be confused with baking, roasting usually involves cooking food at a higher temperature than most baked recipes.

In the previous chapter, I used the **Stewing** method for my oxtails. To stew is to cook food for a long time in a covered pot with liquid over low heat. Usually, the liquid in the pot is brought to a boil, then it's covered, and the heat is reduced, so the mixture simmers. This moist-cooking technique helps tough cuts of meat become tender. When you want low-and-slow, ultra-tender meat, turn to stew. **Pressure cooking** is also in the same family as stewing; however you can reduce your cooking time drastically. Thanks to an airtight gasket seal that traps steam, pressure cookers can cook food quicker and more evenly than pretty much any other method. The airtight seal allows intense pressure and heat to build up inside the cooker.

BRAISING sounds like it could be an intimidating cooking method, but it's much easier than you think. To braise is to cook foods in a small amount of liquid in a tightly covered pan on the stovetop or in the oven. Less-tender cuts of meat like pot roast are perfect for braising because they allow all juices and flavors to seep in and tenderize the meat.

People think of vegetables when it comes to **Steaming**. To steam is to cook foods over boiling water. The steam from the water cooks food without washing away any color or nutrients. Food is placed in a steamer basket, set over boiling water, and covered. Vegetables in general, do not take long to cook. Although you can steam rice, dumplings, and other items, I will save that for another book.

As you can see, I have

a passion for food that supersedes my love for creating but also lends itself to bringing humans together. I wanted to put together some of my favorite and most requested dinner dishes in this chapter. I hope these recipes inspire you to be creative, deepens the quality time you share with the ones you love, and foster new friendships. Feel free to mix and match my recommended side dishes with some of your favorite dinner recipes or make more than one to have options. Double-check your grocery list, grab your apron and let's get cooking because now you know "What's for Dinner"!

GRILLED ROSEMARY PEPPERCORN LAMBCHOPS

WILTED GARLIC SPINACH & WHIPPED SWEET POTATOES

SERVINGS: 4-6 | PREP: 20 MINS | TOTAL: 45 MINS

INGREDIENTS

FOR THE LAMB

2 pounds lamb chops

4 cloves garlic, minced

1 tablespoon fresh rosemary chopped

1 ¼ teaspoon kosher salt

½ teaspoon chili flakes

½ teaspoon cracked black pepper

1 teaspoon lemon juice

¼ cup olive oil

FOR THE SWEET POTATOES

2-3 sweet potatoes or yams, peeled and small cubed

3 tablespoons butter, room temperature

1 tablespoon brown sugar

1 teaspoon cinnamon

¼ teaspoon nutmeg

Salt to taste

FOR THE SPINACH

2 large bunches of spinach, about 1 pound

Extra virgin olive oil

3 cloves garlic, sliced

Salt to taste

DIRECTIONS

LAMB

1. In a small bowl, combine the garlic, rosemary, salt, pepper, chili flakes, lemon juice, and olive oil. Pour the marinade over the lamb chops, making sure to flip them over to cover them completely. Cover and marinate the chops in the fridge for at least 1 hour or overnight.

2. Grill the lamb chops on medium heat for 7-10 minutes, or until the internal temperature reads 145 degrees (recommended) or 165 degrees for well done.

3. Allow the lamb chops to rest on a plate covered with aluminum foil for 5 minutes before serving.

SWEET POTATOES

1. Steam sweet potatoes until you can easily pierce them with a fork, around 15 minutes. If you don't have a steamer, you can boil the sweet potatoes in a large stockpot in lightly salted water. Strain and place potatoes back into the pot.

2. Remove potatoes from the steamer and place in a large pot, and mash with a potato masher. Add butter, brown sugar, cinnamon, nutmeg, and salt. Beat ingredients into sweet potatoes until thoroughly mixed and fluffy.

3. Add more salt and pepper to taste.

SPINACH

1. If using fresh spinach, cut off the thick stems of the spinach and discard. Clean the spinach by filling up your sink with water and soaking the spinach to loosen any sand or dirt. Drain the spinach, and then repeat soaking and draining. Put the spinach in a salad spinner to remove any excess moisture. For prepackage spinach, you can skip with step.

2. Heat 2 Tbsp olive oil in a large skillet on medium-high heat. Add the garlic and sauté for about 1 minute, until the garlic begins to brown.

3. Add the spinach to the pan, packing it down a bit if you need to with a spatula. Lift the spinach and turn it over in the pan so that you coat more of it with olive oil and garlic. Do this a couple of times. Cover the pan and cook for 1-2 minutes. Turn heat off, uncover and turn the spinach over again, drain off excess liquid.

SHRIMP SCAMPI

SERVINGS: 4 | PREP: 15 MINS | TOTAL: 30 MINS

INGREDIENTS

1 package linguine pasta

3 tablespoons butter

2 tablespoons olive oil

2 shallots, fine diced

3 cloves garlic, minced

1/8 teaspoon chili flakes

1 ½ lb large shrimp, shelled

¾ teaspoon kosher salt, or to taste

Fresh crack pepper

½ cup dry white wine (I used sauvignon blanc)

1 lemon, juiced

1/3 cup parsley, finely chopped

Asiago, fresh shaved (optional garnish)

DIRECTIONS

1. Bring a large pot of salted water to a boil; cook linguine in boiling water until nearly tender, 6 to 8 minutes. Drain.

2. In a large skillet, melt 2 tablespoons butter with olive oil. Add shallots and garlic, and sauté until fragrant, about 1 minute. Add wine, salt, red pepper flakes, and plenty of black pepper, and bring to a simmer. Let the wine reduce by half, about 2 minutes.

3. Add shrimp and remaining butter, sauté until they just turn pink, 2 to 4 minutes, depending upon their size. Stir in the parsley and lemon juice and serve over or toss in the pasta. Garnish with Asiago.

CHEF NOTES

An excellent vegetable to add to this dish is asparagus. You will need 1 lb asparagus trimmed and cut into 2" pieces. After you have cooked your pasta, place a large, deep pan over medium/high heat and add 1 Tbsp olive oil and 1 Tbsp butter. Add asparagus, season lightly with 1/4 tsp salt and 1/8 tsp pepper, and cook uncovered for 5 minutes or until crisp-tender, stirring occasionally. Remove from pan. At this point, use the same pan and start step 2 and add the cooked asparagus in with the parsley and lemon juice.

HERB DE PROVENCE ROASTED CHICKEN

SERVINGS: 4 | PREP: 15 MINS | TOTAL: 50 MINS

INGREDIENTS

One 3 to 4-pound chicken, cut into 8 parts (2 breasts, 2 thighs, 2 legs, 2 wings), excluding the back

¼ cup Extra virgin olive oil

3 tablespoon Herb de Provence

1 tablespoon Kosher salt

2 teaspoons Freshly course black pepper

1 teaspoon lemon zest

1 onion, cut into quarters

1 lb fingerling potatoes, sliced in half lengthwise

2 cloves garlic, minced

1 lb carrots, washed, peeled, and cut

DIRECTIONS

1. Preheat oven to 400 degrees. Line a rimmed 12in x 18in a baking sheet with foil or, even better, parchment paper. Thoroughly wash the potatoes & carrots with a scrubber and cut them into smaller pieces. Pat dry with a paper towel. Trim the chicken pieces of excess fat. Pat the chicken pieces dry with a paper towel.

2. Add chicken, potatoes and, carrots, onion & garlic to the lined rimmed baking dish and sprinkle with herb de Provence, salt, cracked pepper, lemon zest, and garlic. Drizzle with 3-4 tbsp olive oil. Carefully toss everything to coat.

3. Arrange the chicken pieces in the pan so that all the pieces are skin side up, and the largest pieces (the breasts) are in the center of the pan. Don't crowd the pan; allow room in between the pieces.

4. Place in the oven and bake chicken and potatoes for 1 hour, or the internal temperature of the chicken breasts is 165°F. Check for doneness -if the potatoes and chicken thighs are soft and easily pierced with the fork, they are ready. If the chicken and potatoes have not browned up as much as you would like, turn the broil setting on and broil for 5 minutes. Watch carefully, or they will burn.

STREET "TACO TUESDAY" 3 WAYS

SERVINGS: 4 | PREP: 10 MINS | TOTAL: 30 MINS

INGREDIENTS

10 - 15 (6-inch) corn or flour tortillas

GROUND BEEF OR TURKEY

1-pound ground beef or chicken

2 tablespoon olive oil

1 teaspoon ground cumin

1 teaspoon smoked paprika

½ teaspoon garlic powder

½ teaspoon chili powder

½ teaspoon salt

¼ teaspoon cayenne pepper

½ teaspoon freshly cracked pepper

CRISPY FISH OR SHRIMP

1 lb fresh cod, cut into 1-inch (2-cm) thick strips

1 cup all-purpose flour

½ teaspoon baking powder

1 teaspoon salt

1/2 teaspoon ground black pepper

1 cup beer

CHICKEN TINGA

1 tablespoon olive oil

1 cup sweet onion, chopped

2 cloves garlic, minced

1–2 chipotle peppers in adobo sauce, chopped

1 teaspoon dried oregano

1/2 teaspoon ground cumin

3/4 cup canned crushed tomatoes

1/4 cup chicken stock

1/2 teaspoon kosher salt

3 cups shredded cooked chicken

DIRECTIONS

1. **FOR BEEF**- Place a skillet over medium heat. You can add 1 tablespoon of olive oil if you want; however with the meat being fattier it is not necessary. Once the skillet is hot, add the ground beef (if using turkey, I recommend 2 tablespoons of olive oil) and break it apart with a wooden spoon.

2. Cook, stirring and breaking apart the beef often until it begins to brown. Add in the cumin, paprika, garlic powder, chili powder, salt, and pepper. Stir well to disperse all the seasonings. Cook until the beef is just browned.

3. **FOR FISH**- In a large bowl, combine flour, salt, pepper, and baking powder. Add the beer and whisk until smooth. Let sit for 15 minutes.

4. Heat the vegetable oil in a large pot until it reaches 350°F (180°C).

5. Coat the fish in the batter, then transfer to the oil and fry until golden on the outside and cook through for 5-7 minutes. Drain the fish on a wire rack set over a baking sheet lined with paper towels.

6. **FOR CHICKEN**- Heat a large skillet over medium. Once hot, add the oil and onion. Sauté for 4 minutes or until translucent, stirring occasionally. Add in the garlic and cook for 30 seconds more. Stir in the chipotles, oregano, and cumin, and cook for 1 minute. Add in the tomatoes, stock, and salt. Bring to a simmer and cook for 5 -7 minutes.

7. Place your hot ingredients into a blender and puree until smooth. Return sauce to the pan and add chicken, cook for another 5 mins, then taste and adjust seasoning.

TOPPINGS & SAUCES

This is the fun part! There is no right or wrong way to make a "Completed Taco" you can keep it simple, like street tacos with onion, cilantro, and lime, or you go tropical with a pineapple and mango salsa.

It is a personal preference, but I wanted to give you a few options to try and jazz up your tacos.

ASIAN SLAW

1/3 cup rice vinegar

1 tablespoon granulated sugar

1 tablespoon soy sauce

1 teaspoon grated fresh ginger

1 teaspoon chili-garlic sauce

¼ teaspoon kosher salt

¼ teaspoon black pepper

¼ red onion, thin sliced

1 (16-oz.) package tri-color coleslaw mix

¼ cup chopped fresh cilantro

DIRECTIONS

Whisk together rice vinegar, granulated sugar, soy sauce, fresh ginger, chili-garlic sauce, kosher salt, and black pepper. Stir in onions, coleslaw mix, and fresh cilantro.

SRIRACHA AIOLI

1/2 cup sour cream

1/3 cup mayo

2 Tbsp lime juice from 1 medium lime

1 tsp garlic powder

1 tsp onion powder

1 tsp paprika

1 tsp Sriracha sauce or to taste

DIRECTIONS

Combine all sriracha sauce ingredients in a medium bowl and whisk until well blended. Taste and adjust with salt if needed.

PINEAPPLE PICO

1 1/2 cups pineapple, diced fresh

1/4 red bell pepper, chopped

2-3 Tab red onion, small chopped

2 Tab cilantro fresh, chopped

2 tsp jalapeño*, seeds and ribs removed, finely chopped

1 Tab lime juice, or more if needed

Sea salt to taste

DIRECTIONS

In a medium serving bowl, combine the pineapple, bell pepper, onion, cilantro, and jalapeño. Add the lime juice and salt and stir to combine.

RED WINE BRAISED SHORT RIBS

SERVINGS: 6 | PREP: 25 MINS | TOTAL: 4 HOURS, 25 MINS

INGREDIENTS

4-5 lbs bone-in short ribs, at least 1 1/2 inches thick

2 Tab olive oil

Kosher salt and fresh cracked pepper

1 medium onion, large dice

3 garlic cloves, crushed

6 carrots peeled and cut into large chucks

3 Tab tomatoes paste

2 cups red wine (I used McBride Sisters Red Blend)

2 cups beef broth or chicken

3 spring thyme

1 spring rosemary

Parsley for garnish

DIRECTIONS

1. Preheat oven to 300 degrees. Heat oil in a large Dutch oven over medium-high heat. Season short ribs on all sides with salt and pepper. Working in batches, sear short ribs on all sides until deeply and evenly browned, 6 to 8 minutes per batch. Sear ribs on all sides and transfer to a plate. Transfer browned short ribs to a large plate and continue with the remaining ribs.

2. Add onions and carrots to cook, occasionally stirring, until browned about 10 minutes. Add garlic and cook another minute; add tomato paste and cook another 5 minutes. Continue to cook, occasionally stirring, until tomato paste has started to caramelize a bit on the bottom and up the edges of the pot, about 2 to 3 minutes.

3. Add red wine and, using a wooden spoon, scrape up any browned or caramelized bits. Let this simmer for 2 to 3 minutes to take the edge off and reduce a bit. Stir in beef stock along with thyme and rosemary. Turn the heat to low and add back in the short ribs.

4. Bring to a simmer, then cover and transfer to oven. Cover with a lid and bake for 3-4 hours. Cook, undisturbed, until short ribs are meltingly tender and falling off the bone. Let rest for 10 minutes and garnish with parsley.

CHEF NOTES

I recommend serving this dish with whipped mashed potatoes, roasted garlic polenta, or traditional white rice.

SALMON FLORENTINE WITH RICE PILAF

SERVINGS: 4 | PREP: 5 MINS | TOTAL: 25 MINS

INGREDIENTS

- 4 Salmon filets (skin optional) 6-8 oz each
- 2 Tab olive oil
- 3 garlic cloves, minced
- 1 Tab Italian seasoning
- ¼ cup sundried tomatoes, julienne
- 1 cup fresh spinach
- 3 Tab lemon juice
- ¼ cup white wine
- ½ heavy cream
- Salt & fresh cracked pepper
- ½ tsp red chili flakes (optional)

DIRECTIONS

1. In a large nonstick pan, heat olive oil. Season salmon with a bit of salt and pepper, add salmon to the pan, skin side up. Let skin brown for about 3-4 mins, flip and let salmon skin crisp, another 3-4 minutes. Remove from pan and set aside.

2. Add garlic, sundried tomatoes, and Italian season to the pan. Sauté for 3-4 mins, add in wine and lemon juice bring to a simmer, stirring often. Turn heat down to low and slowly add in the cream; whisk until evenly combined, about 5-7 mins. Return heat to medium-high and add salmon back to the pan; top with spinach.

3. Cover with a lid and let the spinach wilt and the salmon is fully cooked, ladling sauce over fish to help the salmon cook. When the sauce thickens and salmon is cooked through, remove it from heat and sprinkle with chili flakes.

RICE PILAF

INGREDIENTS

2 tablespoons butter

1/2 cup orzo pasta

1/2 cup onion diced

2 cloves garlic minced

½ tsp dried thyme

½ tsp dried oregano

1/2 cup long white grain rice uncooked

2 cups chicken broth (or vegetable broth)

1 tsp Salt

DIRECTIONS

1. In a large skillet over medium heat, melt butter and add orzo pasta until golden brown. Once golden add in onion and until onion becomes translucent. Add garlic and cook for another minute or two until fragrant.

2. Add the rice to the pan and stir to coat with butter. Add in chicken broth, salt, thyme, and oregano, bring to a boil. Once boiling, reduce heat to medium-low, cover skillet with a lid, and simmer until the rice is tender and the liquid has absorbed 30 to 25 minutes.

3. Remove from heat and let stand for 5 minutes. Taste and adjust seasoning as needed.

CHEF NOTES

A GOOD BRAND IS NEAR EAST RICE PILAF: If you do not like to make rice pilaf from scratch. If you would like an additional vegetable, roasted broccolini, caramelized onions, green beans, or zucchini.

CAJUN PORK TENDERLOIN
HASSLE BACK SWEET POTATO & GREEN BEANS

SERVINGS: 6 | PREP: 10 MINS | TOTAL: 35 MINS

INGREDIENTS

2 Tab olive oil

2 Tab smoked paprika

2 ½ Tab kosher salt

2 Tab garlic powder

1 Tab ground black pepper

1 Tab onion powder

2 Tab Italian seasoning

1 Tab cayenne pepper

HASSELBACK SWEET POTATOE

6 medium sweet potatoes

6 Tab butter, room temperature

4 garlic cloves, minced

1 Tab ground cinnamon

1 tsp ground nutmeg

½ tsp kosher salt

2 Tab brown sugar

GREEN BEANS

1 lb fresh green beans, trimmed

2 Tab olive oil

¼ cup yellow onion, diced

¾ tsp onion powder

¾ tsp garlic powder

¾ tsp kosher salt

Black pepper to taste

DIRECTIONS

FOR THE PORK: Preheat the oven to 425°F. Stir together the oil, paprika, oregano, onion flakes, thyme, garlic powder, cayenne, 11/4 teaspoons salt, and 1/2 teaspoon pepper. Rub the spice mixture all over the tenderloins and place them on a foil-lined baking pan.

2. Roast the tenderloins until browned and just pink in the center (145°F on an instant-read thermometer), about 25 minutes. Let stand 5-7 minutes before serving.

FOR THE POTATO: Preheat the oven to 425 degrees. Line a baking sheet with aluminum foil and spray with nonstick cooking spray: Wash and dry potatoes. Make a series of 1/8-inch slices along the top of each potato, stopping 1/2 inch from the bottom.

2. In a medium-sized bowl, take butter, cinnamon, nutmeg, brown sugar, and salt and mix. Brush the potatoes (including the bottoms) and between the slices with half of the butter.

3. Bake sweet potatoes on a prepared baking sheet for 40-50 minutes, then remove from oven. Brush baked potatoes with any remaining butter accumulated at the pan's bottom.

FOR THE GREEN BEANS: Heat olive oil in a skillet over medium heat; add onions and cook for 2-3 minutes, then stir green beans, onion powder, garlic powder, salt, and black pepper together until desired tenderness is reached, 5 to 10 minutes.

CHEF NOTES

The Hassel back potatoes will take at least 50 mins to bake, so you would want to start this step in advance; therefore, your pork tenderloin and potatoes will be done around the same time. You should start your green beans while your pork is resting and your sweet potatoes are about to come out of the oven.

FAJITA LOADED BAKED POTATO
BROCCOLI & CHEESE

SERVINGS: 4 | PREP: 10 MINS | TOTAL: 50 MINS

INGREDIENTS

- 4 russet potatoes
- 2 cups cooked chopped chicken, beef, or pork (your preference)
- 2 tablespoons olive oil
- 2 teaspoons salt
- ½ red bell pepper, julienne
- ½ green bell pepper, julienne
- ½ white onion, julienne
- 2 Tbsp all-purpose flour
- 1/4 tsp onion powder
- 1/8 tsp garlic powder
- 1 cup cheddar cheese, plus more for topping
- 1 1/2 cup broccoli, chopped and steamed
- 1 teaspoon pepper
- ¼ cup milk
- Bacon, cooked and chopped (optional)
- sour cream (optional)
- chive (optional)

DIRECTIONS

1. Heat to 400 degrees. Pierce each potato several times with a fork. Place potatoes in the oven and bake until potatoes are tender, about 45 minutes to 1 hour.

2. In a medium skillet on high heat add olive oil, peppers, and onions and sauté for 5 mins, then add pre-cooked meat, cook for another 2-4 minutes, and set aside.

3. For the broccoli cheese sauce: In a small or medium saucepan, melt butter over medium heat. Add onion powder, garlic powder, and flour and cook, constantly whisking, 1 minute. While whisking, pour in milk, season with salt and pepper to taste and allow the mixture to cook, continually stirring, until it boils and the mixture has thickened. Reduce to warm heat and stir in cheddar cheese. Stir until cheese has melted, then stir in ½ cup steamed broccoli.

4. Turn oven onto broil. Split the potato in ½ but do not go all the way through; use a fork to fluff the potato. Ladle a couple of spoons full of the broccoli cheese sauce into the potato, evenly distribute your sautéed peppers and meat, and remaining steamed broccoli, then top with extra cheddar cheese. Placed loaded potatoes on a parchment paper-lined baking sheet and broil in oven for 3-5 minutes or until the cheese is melted and bubbly. Remove from oven and let stand for 5-7 minutes before serving; top with sour cream, chives, and bacon.

INGREDIENTS

FIG, BRIE & PROSCIUTTO

6 Black mission figs, sliced into quarters

2 Naan flatbreads (I used Stonefire)

3 tablespoons extra virgin olive oil, divided

8 oz Brie cheese, sliced

2 oz prosciutto, sliced thin

2 oz baby arugula leaves

1 Tab honey (optional)

1 oz walnuts (optional)

Balsamic glaze

Kosher salt

Freshly ground black pepper (optional)

TRI-COLOR CHERRY TOMATO, SPINACH & GARLIC

1-pint cherry tomatoes halved

3 garlic cloves, minced

1 teaspoon dried Italian seasoning

½ teaspoon kosher salt

1/2 teaspoon black pepper

2 tablespoons olive oil, plus more for storage

1 cups spinach

¼ cup marinara

2 tablespoon olive oil

1 cups mozzarella cheese shredded

1 cup parmesan, shredded

2 Flatbreads

fresh basil for garnish

BBQ CHICKEN

¼ cup your favorite BBQ sauce

½ cup cooked chicken, shredded or chopped

1 small red onion, julienne

grated smoked Gouda

Grated mozzarella

Cilantro

NAAN "FLATBREAD" PIZZA
3 SAUCES 3 WAYS

SERVINGS: 4-6 | PREP: 15 MINS | TOTAL: 30 MINS

DIRECTIONS

Preheat oven to 450 degrees. If using a pizza stone, lightly oil and place in the oven to heat up. If using a baking sheet, lightly oil it and set it aside. Pre-toast your naan flatbread in the oven for 5-7 minutes if you want a crispy pizza.

FOR THE FIG & BRIE: Drizzle 1 tablespoon of olive oil on each flatbread. Top brie slices, fig slices, and prosciutto evenly. I tear the prosciutto into about 3" pieces with my hands. Bake for 10-15 minutes until cheese is melted, prosciutto is slightly crispy, and naan is golden brown.

Remove from oven and top each pizza with about a ½ cup of arugula, walnuts, honey, and cracked pepper. Drizzle with balsamic if using.

FOR TOMATO & SPINACH: Slice cherry tomatoes in half and toss with fresh minced garlic, olive oil, Italian seasoning blend, parsley, and salt. Spread onto a sheet pan lined with parchment paper or rubbed with oil (to avoid sticking) in one single layer. Set timer for 15 min and roast for 15-20 minutes total.

While tomatoes are roasting, heat a small pan to medium heat and wilt spinach for a minute or so in oil until bright green and soft. Set aside. Spread naan flatbread with marinara and top with grated mozzarella and Parmesan. Top with wilted spinach and roasted tomatoes and bake for 10-12 minutes or until your naan is crispy and cheese is melted.

FOR BBQ CHICKEN: Mix 2-3 tablespoons of the barbecue sauce with the chicken.

Place the naan on a rimmed baking sheet. Top each naan flatbread with the remaining BBQ sauce, followed by the cheese, chicken, BBQ sauce mixture, and sliced onion.

Bake for 10-15 minutes in the lower part of the oven, or until cheese is melted and the crust is browned. Top each pizza with one tablespoon of chopped fresh cilantro.

GREEN CHILI CHICKEN ENCHILADAS

SERVINGS: 4 | PREP: 20 MINS | TOTAL: 40 MINS

INGREDIENTS

2 cups chicken, cooked and shredded

2 cups Monterey jack cheese, shredded

1 Tab Chili powder

1 cup Mexican- blend shredded cheese

19 oz green chile enchilada sauce

1 cup sour cream

1 small white onion, peeled and small diced

8 medium flour tortillas (you can use corn)

4 oz can green chiles, chopped

salt and pepper

OPTIONAL TOPPINGS

fresh cilantro, chopped red onions, diced avocado, avocado, sour cream, and/or crumbled cotija cheese

DIRECTIONS

1. Preheat oven to 350°F. Prepare your enchilada sauce.

2. In a small bowl, combine chicken, 2 cups Monterey cheese, chili powder, green chiles, salt, and pepper. To assemble the enchiladas, set up an assembly line including tortillas, enchilada sauce, chicken mixture, and cheese. Layout a tortilla and spread two tablespoons of sauce over the surface of the tortilla. Add a generous spoonful of the chicken mixture in a line down the center of the tortilla, then sprinkle with 1/3 cup cheese. Roll up tortilla and place in a greased 9 x 13-inch baking dish.

3. Assemble the remaining enchiladas. Spoon 2 tablespoons of sour cream down the center of each tortilla, then spread any remaining sauce evenly over the top of the enchiladas, followed by Mexican blended cheese.

4. Bake uncovered for 20 minutes until the enchiladas are cooked through, and the tortillas are slightly crispy on the outside. Remove pan from the oven and serve the enchiladas while they are nice and warm, garnished with your choice of toppings.

CHEF NOTES

For those of you who enjoy red enchilada sauce, you can easily replace it; it's all a matter of personal preference. Also, if you are using corn tortillas, you will need to take a small skillet, bring enchilada sauce to boil. Remove from heat. Dip each tortilla into the heated sauce for a few seconds to soften, and follow the steps to stuff and roll the enchiladas.

INGREDIENTS

HIBACHI RICE

2 cups previously cooked long-grain white rice, cool to the touch

¼ cup carrots, finely chopped

¼ cup peas

1 egg, beaten

½ cup white onion, chopped

4 tablespoons canola oil

12 tablespoons soy sauce

3 teaspoons sesame oil

6 tablespoons butter

salt

pepper

HIBACHI CHICKEN, STEAK, OR SHRIMP

1 lb chicken breast cut into bite-sized pieces

2 tsp lemon juice fresh

Or 1b shrimp, peeled and deveined

Or 1 lb Sirloin steak, cubed

1 Tablespoon Teriyaki sauce

Garlic powder, as needed

Onion powder, as needed

Paprika, as needed

HIBACHI VEGETABLES

1 zucchini large, quartered, and cut into 2" pieces

1 white onion large, halved, and cut into 1/2" pieces

2 cups baby Bella mushrooms about 8 ounces, quartered

YUM YUM SAUCE

1½ cup Mayonnaise

1 tsp garlic powder

½ tsp Paprika

½ tsp Sriracha

½ tsp Cayenne pepper

1 Tab rice wine vinegar

1 Tab water, as needed

1/2- 1 Tab ketchup

HIBACHI FRIED RICE
YUM YUM SAUCE

SERVINGS: 6 | PREP: 15 MINS | TOTAL: 40 MINS

CHEF NOTES

Depending on your comfort level, you can cook your choice of meat and vegetables simultaneously. If you are doing all three types of meat or two, you can use the same pan to cook the meats; be sure not to burn the bottom of the pan or you will have to use a new pan for each meat. I would recommend double or tripling the Yum Yum sauce recipe if you know your family or guest like extra sauce.

DIRECTIONS

YUM YUM SAUCE: Mix all the Yum Yum sauce ingredients (except water) together. Add water in small amounts at a time until you reach your desired sauce consistency. Chill in the fridge.

FOR THE FRIED RICE: Heat 2 tablespoons avocado oil on medium-high in a large skillet or wok. Add diced onion, frozen vegetables, and sauté until onions are almost translucent for about 3 minutes. Move the vegetables to the side of the pan.

2. Take beaten egg and scramble with a spatula until cooked through and thoroughly scrambled. Add cooked rice and 4 Tab butter. Cook for 5 minutes and stir frequently. Add 4 tablespoons soy sauce and cook 1 additional minute. Put rice in a bowl and pack it to keep hot.

FOR THE CHICKEN: Heat 1 1/2 teaspoons sesame oil and 1 tablespoon canola oil in the same skillet or wok used for fried rice. Add chicken, 3 tablespoons soy sauce, 1 tablespoon butter, lemon juice, salt, and pepper to the skillet. Cook chicken until it is no longer pink, about 5-7 minutes. Stir only once or twice so chicken will brown.

FOR STEAK AND/OR SHRIMP: Season the steak or/and shrimp with kosher salt, pepper, garlic powder, paprika, and onion powder. Heat canola oil in a skillet over medium-high heat.

2. Add in the steak and/or shrimp and sear on both sides for about 3-4 minutes until cooked through, then a couple of teaspoons of Teriyaki sauce and sesame oil. Remove from the pan and keep warm.

FOR THE VEGETABLES: In a separate large skillet or wok, heat 1 1/2 teaspoons sesame oil and 1 tablespoon avocado oil on medium-high heat. Add sliced onion, baby portabella mushrooms, zucchini, 1 tablespoon butter, salt, and pepper to skillet. Sauté until vegetables are tender, about 6-8 minutes.

THE ULTIMATE CRAB BOIL
"TRIPLE THREAT SAUCE"

SERVINGS: 6-8 | PREP: 20 MINS | TOTAL: 40 MINS

INGREDIENTS

5 clusters Snow crab legs, washed thoroughly

1 lb Shrimp, deveined, tail on

1 lb Andouille sausage (pork or chicken), cut into thick slices

6 Corn on the cob

6 Baby red potatoes

3 Tab Garlic, diced

2 sticks Butter

1/4 cup Olive oil

6 Tab Old Bay seasoning

1 whole Lemon, juiced

2 Tab lemon pepper seasoning

2 Tab Cajun seasoning

2 tsp chili flakes

3 Bay leaves

TRIPLE THREAT SAUCE

4 sticks Butter

5 Tab Garlic, diced

1 Lemon, juiced

1 Tab Old Bay seasoning

2 Tab Cajun seasoning

2 tsp Red pepper flakes

3 Tab Lemon pepper seasoning

½ cup seafood broth from boil (optional)

DIRECTIONS

1. Fill up a large stockpot with water, leaving enough room at the top to add the seafood. Add old bay seasoning, lemon, lemon pepper, Cajun seasoning, and bay leaves. Bring to a light boil. Place corn and potatoes into the seasoned water. Boil for 10 minutes. Add the crab legs and sausage. Cover with a lid and boil for an additional 15 minutes.

2. Add the shrimp. Boil for 5-7 minutes depending on size (do not overcook).

3. Melt one stick of butter in a skillet on medium heat, add garlic and sauté for 30 seconds, constantly stirring so the garlic does not burn. Add the juice of the lemon, and all the seasonings. Adjust cayenne and red pepper to your level of spiciness. Add remaining 3 sticks of butter. Simmer until butter is melted, stirring constantly.

4. If using seafood broth, gently stir it into the mixture now. Drain the water and remove bay leaves—transfer to serving dish or leave in the stockpot.

5. Pour that delicious garlic butter sauce all over, and/or reserve some sauce on the side to dip the seafood in. Enjoy!

CHEF NOTES

Seafood broth is used to "cut" the sauce. It does not take away from the flavor in any way. It's great to add broth if trying to create more sauce or pour directly over your seafood boil.

PAN-SEARED HALIBUT
LEMON CAPER SAUCE

SERVINGS: 2 | PREP: 10 MINS | TOTAL: 30 MINS

INGREDIENTS

1 lb fresh halibut, cut into 2 equal portions (skinned* optional)

3 Tab butter, divided

2 Tab olive oil

Kosher salt

Fresh cracked pepper

2 tsp fresh garlic, minced

½ cup white wine (I used Chardonnay)

2 Tab shallots, minced

1 tsp lemon zest

1 Tab lemon juice, fresh

2 Tab capers, drained

Parsley, chopped (optional garnish)

DIRECTIONS

1. Take your fish and dry the flesh between two paper towels to help remove as much moisture from the surface as possible. Preheat a large skillet with two tablespoons of butter and olive oil. Season fish with salt and pepper; once the butter mixture starts to slightly brown, add the fish presentation side down. Carefully press the flesh with a fish spatula to create direct contact with the oil to create a golden crust.

2. Cook for 5 minutes, gently flip over, being careful not to splash hot oil, and cook for another 3-5 minutes. Using your fish spatula, remove fish to a plate. Pour off all but two tablespoons of the fat left in the pan. Best to pour it all into a bowl, let the burned bits sink to the bottom, then skim off a few tablespoons of the fat at the top and place it back into the pan.

3. Keep the heat at medium, add the shallots and garlic, and cook for one minute. Add the wine and cook to evaporate. Then add the lemon juice, zest, and capers. Cook for a minute, then remove from heat and stir in the remaining tablespoon of butter and stir to make the sauce.

4. Put the fish back into the pan along with any liquid from the plate, bring the heat back to medium heat and use the spoon to ladle the sauce over the top cook for approximately 30 seconds, turn off the heat and garnish with parsley and lemon slice.

CHEF NOTES

This dish pairs well with quinoa salad, couscous, or rice. Sautéed or roasted asparagus and/or broccolini. I chose chardonnay wine to cook with for this dish because the butter notes in the wine help bring out the flavors in the fish. *** See wine pairing notes in "Its 5'oclock Somewhere."

GRILLED CHICKEN BRUSCHETTA

SERVINGS: 4 | PREP: 35 MINS | TOTAL: 50 MINS

INGREDIENTS

4 boneless skinless chicken breasts

1/4 cup olive oil

2 Tab lemon juice

1 tsp salt

1 tsp Italian seasoning

½ tsp garlic powder

½ tsp onion powder

1/2 teaspoon pepper

4 slices buffalo mozzarella cheese

FOR BRUSCHETTA

1 1/2 cups cherry tomatoes, halved

1/2 tsp garlic finely minced

1 Tab olive oil

1/4 cup basil leaves, chiffonade

salt and pepper to taste

2 tablespoons red onion, minced

Balsamic glaze

DIRECTIONS

1. In a large bowl, mix the olive oil, lemon juice, salt, Italian seasoning, garlic powder, onion powder, and pepper. Add the chicken breasts and marinate for at least 30 minutes or overnight.

2. Preheat a grill or grill pan to medium-high. Remove the chicken from the marinade and place it on the grill. Cook for 5-10 minutes (depending on the thickness of the breast) on each side or until done. Place the cheese slices on top of the chicken. Cover the grill and cook until cheese is melted, 2-3 minutes.

3. While the chicken is cooking, make the bruschetta topping. In a medium bowl, combine the tomatoes, garlic, olive oil, red onion, basil, salt, and pepper. Let stand for 10 minutes. Spoon the bruschetta mixture over the chicken. Drizzle with balsamic glaze and serve.

CHEF NOTES

If you are not in the mood to grill or don't have a grill, then preheat your oven to 425 degrees. Follow the above steps to make bruschetta and complete your chicken. Use the same marinating steps. Place chicken in a 9x13 baking dish and bake for 25-30 mins or until the chicken reaches 165 degrees. I recommend serving with chicken over a bed of linguini or with some garlic mashed potatoes. However, this would also be a great compliment to a salad.

ITALIAN STUFFED SHELLS

SERVINGS: 8 | PREP: 25 MINS | TOTAL: 1 HOUR

INGREDIENTS

¾ lb ground turkey (or beef)

2 Tab olive oil

2 Tab Italian seasoning

2 tsp garlic powder

1 tsp kosher salt

1 small yellow onion, diced

10 ounces jumbo pasta shells

16 ounces whole-milk ricotta cheese

1/2 cup Romano cheese, grated

12 leaves fresh basil, cut into chiffonade

Freshly ground black pepper

8 ounces Parmesan, grated

2 jars of good-quality marinara sauce

8 ounces mozzarella cheese, grated

Kosher salt

DIRECTIONS

1. Preheat the oven to 350 degrees F. Bring a large pot of salted water to a boil. Add the pasta shells and cook for half the cooking time on the package; make sure not to overcook. Drain and rinse in cool water. Set aside.

2. In a large sauté pan, heat on medium-high the olive oil and onions, cook for 3-4 minutes. Add ground turkey, Italian seasoning, salt, and garlic powder. Cook turkey for 7-10 minutes until brown throughout, and then add in marinara sauce, bring to a simmer for 5 minutes and remove from heat.

3. Mix the ricotta, Romano, basil, some salt and pepper, and half of the Parmesan in a bowl. Stir until combined.

4. To assemble, coat the bottom of a baking dish with some sauce. Fill each half-cooked shell with about 2-3 tablespoons of the turkey marinara and the cheese mixture, then place face-down on the sauce. Repeat with the shells until the cheese mixture is gone. Top the shells with the remaining sauce. Sprinkle on the mozzarella and extra Parmesan.

5. Bake for 20 to 25 minutes until bubbly, then broil for 2-5 minutes or until the cheese browns.

NEXT

EAT YOUR VEGETABLES!
VEGETARIAN & VEGAN MEALS DONE RIGHT.

AT HOME WITH
Chef Mark Phillips

EAT YOUR VEGETABLES!

I specifically wanted to dedicate an entire chapter to vegetable-based meals; why you ask? On my continuous journey of learning and cooking with food, I have found that what was once a stigma about being a vegetarian or vegan has elevated into a long, lucrative lifestyle. Let me start by explaining the difference between vegan and vegetarian. Veganism is currently defined as a way of living that attempts to exclude all forms of animal exploitation and cruelty, be it from food, clothing, or any other purpose. There is a broad spectrum. The simplest definition of vegetarianism is a diet free of animals. Lacto-Ovo vegetarians avoid animal flesh but eat eggs and milk products. So, it boils down to an induvial preference.

It is important to me as a chef to be as well versed in the culinary field, and with the growing trend of adding more vegetables into one's diet, I wanted to share more exciting and creative ways to add vegetables into anyone's life. Over the years, I have also begun adding more vegetarian and vegan meals into my daily or weekly meals. Like some of you, I was like, OMG, how am I going to get full and be satisfied with no meat? Luckily, I am here to help you start that journey or provide some exciting recipes for those who are already about that vegetable life.

Whether you want to add one of these recipes as the main course or in the beginning stages and select these recipes as a side, you can't go wrong. Many studies agree that a vegetarian diet can offer a range of health benefits. On a healthier note, vegetarians appear to have lower low-density lipoprotein cholesterol levels, lower blood pressure, and lower rates of hypertension and type 2 diabetes than meat-eaters. Vegetarians also tend to have a lower body mass index, lower overall cancer rates, and lower risk of chronic disease. However, I am no health professional, but I can attest to my personally seeing the benefits of increasing vegetables in my life.

Fasting is the willful refrain from eating for a period. Several times throughout the year, I will go on a fast or do an internal reset on my body by either removing all meat from my daily meal consumption or only eating meat on the weekends as a treat. I know many people do fast for religious or health reasons; either way, I would consult your doctor for any drastic changes in your diet. Eating meat on the weekend usually lasts for months, more like a lifestyle adjustment that helps me crave vegetables even more. Some of my clients (current and past) have special requests, like my baked sweet potato with chipotle chicken peas and broccoli pesto. Another popular vegan meal is my take on Thai coconut curry packed with vegetables and brown rice noodles. Those two are just the tip of the iceberg, but I hope you will enjoy cooking and "Eating Your Vegetables" differently.

The recipes in this chapter are designed to help the everyday individual or family learn more creative ways to prepare meals that do not have any meat in them or little to no animal byproducts. I know cheese or dairy can be one of the most challenging items to take out of anyone's diet, so I wanted to offer vegan and vegetarian options. Let's face it we all have to start somewhere, so grab your apron, get your ingredients together and let's get cooking!

GOUDA CAULIFLOWER MACARONI & CHEESE

SERVINGS: 8 | PREP: 10 MINS | TOTAL: 25 MINS

INGREDIENTS

1 lb steam al dente cauliflower; rough chopped

1 tsp salt

½ tsp fresh cracked pepper

1 Tab chopped garlic

4 Tab salted butter

1 ½ cups Gouda Cheese freshly grated

1 cup white cheddar freshly grated

½ cup Parmesan Cheese crumbled

¾ cups whole Milk

1 ½ cup heavy cream

DIRECTIONS

1. Pre-heat oven to 375 degrees. Bring about 1/4 inch of water to a boil in a large frying pan.

2. Add about 1/2 teaspoon fine sea salt and cleaned cauliflower florets. Cover and steam until as tender as you like (about 3 minutes for crisp-tender and up to 8 minutes for thoroughly cooked, soft florets).

3. Drain any water from cauliflower before using. While cauliflower is draining, mix all cheese together in a separate bowl. In a medium saucepan, place butter and garlic sauté for 2-3 minutes. Slowly add in milk and heavy cream. Bring to a slight boil.

4. Gradually add your cheese into the cream mixture until becoming a thick creamy sauce. Season with salt and pepper, and add cauliflower. Pour cauliflower mac and cheese into an oven-safe baking dish.

TOPPING

1/2 cup panko breadcrumbs

1 tbsp melted butter

1 tbsp parsley; chopped

2 tsp thyme; chopped

TOPPING: Melt butter, then stir everything together. Once thoroughly mixed, you can sprinkle over the top before baking. Bake oven for 20-30 minutes if a family portion or 15 minutes for individual portions.

THAI COCONUT CURRY VEGETABLES & NOODLES

SERVINGS: 4 | PREP: 15 MINS | TOTAL: 30 MINS

INGREDIENTS

2 Tbs coconut oil

2 cloves garlic, minced

1 Tbs fresh ginger, grated

1 4oz can Thai red curry paste (less depending on spice level)

1 small sweet potato

1 bunch fresh baby spinach, rinsed

¼ cup zucchini, sliced

½ cup cremini mushrooms, sliced

4 cups vegetable

1 13oz. can coconut milk

½ Tbs fish sauce (optional)

½ Tbs brown sugar

½ pack rice vermicelli noodles

GARNISH

½ white onion, thin julienne

1 lime, sliced into wedges

1 handful fresh cilantro, rough chopped

Garlic chili paste (optional)

DIRECTIONS

1. Over medium heat add the coconut oil to a large soup pot along with the minced garlic, grated ginger, and all Thai red curry paste except 1 tablespoon. Sauté the garlic, ginger, and curry paste for 1-2 minutes.

2. Add the diced sweet potato and vegetable broth. Bring the pot to a boil over medium-high heat, then reduce the heat to low and let simmer for 5-7 minutes, or until the sweet potatoes are tender. While the soup is simmering, bring a small pot of water to a boil for the vermicelli. Once boiling, add the vermicelli and boil for 2-3 minutes, or just until tender. Drain the rice noodles in a colander and set aside.

3. Once the sweet potatoes are tender, add the coconut milk, fish sauce, zucchini, mushrooms, and brown sugar to the soup. Stir, taste, and adjust the brown sugar and red curry paste if needed. Finally, add the spinach and let them wilt in the hot soup. To serve, divide the rice vermicelli among four bowls. Ladle the soup and vegetables over the noodles, then top with onion, cilantro, a wedge or two of lime, and for extra spice, you can add garlic chili paste or sriracha.

CHEF NOTES

The fish sauce in this recipe lends itself to a more authentic Thai dish; however, I know the smell can be off-putting, so you can omit it if you choose. Also, if you are a fan of bok choy, you can replace instead of spinach, be sure to wash it thoroughly. Chop into one-inch strips, separating the fibrous stalks from the delicate green ends.

ROASTED RED PEPPER HUMMUS WRAP

SERVINGS: 2 | PREP: 5 MINS | TOTAL: 5 MINS

INGREDIENTS

2 tortillas (I used spinach)

2/3 cup red pepper hummus

4-6 slices cucumber, sliced lengthwise

2 leaves of Leafy lettuce, washed and dry

¼ cup carrots, shredded

½ avocado, sliced

½ small red onion, thin sliced

1 Roma tomato, sliced thin

½ cup purple cabbage, shredded

1 Tab olive oil (optional)

DIRECTIONS

1. Spread the hummus on the bottom 1/3 of the wrap, about 1/2 inch from the bottom edge but spreading out the side edges. Layer the cucumber, leafy lettuce, tomato slices, avocado slices, cabbage, carrots, and onions, and drizzle the olive oil.

2. Fold the wrap tightly, as you would a burrito, tucking in all the veggies with the first roll, then rolling firmly to the end. Cut in half and enjoy.

CHEF NOTES

Feel free to switch out any vegetables to make the wrap your own. There is no wrong way to make a wrap! I would also suggest a whole grain wrap, gluten-free, or using collard leaves if you do not want any grain at all.

MUSHROOM BOLOGNESE PASTA

SERVINGS: 4 | PREP: 15 MINS | TOTAL: 35 MINS

INGREDIENTS

2 Tab extra-virgin olive oil

2 Tab butter, salted or unsalted

1 cup onion, about 1 medium onion, chopped

1 stalk celery, finely chopped

1 carrot, peels and finely chopped

¼ pound cremini mushrooms, chopped

½ lb baby Bella mushrooms, chopped

½ lb shiitake mushroom, chopped

Kosher salt

1 Tab finely chopped garlic

¼ cup tomato paste

1 tsp dried oregano leaves

¼ cup red wine, such as malbec

1 cup vegetable broth

1 cup crushed canned tomatoes

2 tsp chopped fresh thyme

½ rigatoni pasta

¼ freshly grated Parmesan cheese (or vegan Parmesan)

DIRECTIONS

1. Bring a large pot of water to a boil and add 2 tablespoons salt and finish cooking pasta according to the directions on the box. Heat the oil and butter in a large skillet or Dutch oven pot over medium heat. When the butter stops foaming, add the carrots, onions, and celery. Cook until softened, about 5 minutes. Stir in the mushrooms and 1 teaspoon salt. Cook another 5 minutes, or until the mushrooms have absorbed their liquid.

2. Add the garlic, oregano, tomato paste and cook for a few seconds until fragrant. Pour in the wine and let it bubble. Add the broth, tomatoes, and thyme, stirring it all together. Bring to a simmer, lower the heat to medium-low and cook 10-12 minutes, until the sauce is thickened.

3. While the sauce cooks, cook the pasta according to package directions, until al dente. Drain.

4. Transfer the pasta to the skillet, stirring to coat with the sauce. Taste for seasoning and add more salt if needed. Sprinkle with the cheese and serve.

GREEK BARLEY BOWL

SERVINGS: 2 | PREP: 20 MINS | TOTAL: 20 MINS

INGREDIENTS

1 cup barley, cooked according to package

1 can chickpea, drained and rinsed

1 cup cherry tomatoes, halved

½ English cucumber diced

6 oz marinated Artichoke Hearts, Quartered

½ cup kalamata olives

½ cup feta cheese

2 cups arugula

FOR DRESSING

1/4 cup olive oil

1 teaspoon dijon mustard

1 tablespoon red wine vinegar

½ teaspoon honey

2 tablespoons lemon juice

1/4 teaspoon garlic powder

1/4 teaspoon onion powder

1/2 teaspoon dried oregano

salt and pepper to taste

1 tablespoon chopped fresh parsley

DIRECTIONS

1. Divide the barley, arugula, chickpea, cherry tomatoes, cucumber, chickpeas, olive, Artichoke, and feta cheese evenly among bowls. For the dressing: combine all ingredients in a small bowl and whisk until combined.

2. Drizzle the dressing over the salad and serve.

BAKED SWEET POTATO & BROCCOLI PESTO w/ CHIPOTLE CHICKPEAS

SERVINGS: 2 | PREP: 10 MINS | TOTAL: 35 MINS

INGREDIENTS

2 medium sweet potatoes

1 cup broccoli florets, steamed al dente

8-10 basil leaves

2 Tbsp olive oil (or avocado oil)

¾ cup chickpeas; drained and rinsed

1/2 cup vegetable stock

1 Tab chipotle seasoning

1 Tab garlic, chopped

1 tsp pine nuts (optional)

1 Tab vegan parmesan (I used Follow Your Heart)

Salt & Pepper

¼ cup cherry tomatoes halved (optional)

DIRECTIONS

1. Preheat oven to 425 degrees. Spray or drizzle a baking sheet with a little bit of oil, then cut sweet potatoes into halves and place skin-side down. Bake 20-25 minutes, or until soft.

2. While the potatoes are baking, blend the broccoli, garlic, Parmesan, pine nuts, basil, oil, salt, and pepper, to create the pesto. Set aside.

3. In a medium-size pot, sauté the chickpeas over medium heat with coconut oil and chipotle seasoning for about 5 minutes, and then add vegetable stock. Bring to a boil for 5-10 mins and then remove from heat.

4. Top each sweet potato, chickpeas, pesto, and tomato. Serve warm, and enjoy!

CAULIFLOWER FRIED RICE

SERVINGS: 4 | PREP: 10 MINS | TOTAL: 25 MINS

INGREDIENTS

½ Tab olive or coconut oil

2 large eggs, beaten

Salt

½ cup chopped scallions, light and green parts separated

½ cup yellow onion, diced

3 garlic cloves, minced

1 Tab finely chopped fresh ginger, from a 1-inch knob

3 cups cauliflower (I use a cheese grater or food processor)

4-5 tablespoons soy sauce (use gluten-free if needed)

1/4 teaspoon crushed red pepper flakes

1 cup frozen peas and carrots

½ cup corn (frozen or fresh)

¼ cup red bell pepper, small diced

1 tsp toasted sesame oil

DIRECTIONS

1. In a large pan, onions for 2-3 minutes in olive oil on a medium/high heat, until onions become soft and transparent the add garlic and sauté for another minute. Next add in peppers, corn, peas, and carrots and cook until carrots begin to soften, and peas are heated for about 3-4 minutes

2. Next stir in scrambled eggs, cauliflower, green onion, crushed red pepper flakes, and soy sauce. Cook stirring frequently for about 5-7 more minutes.

CHEF NOTES

For those of you looking for the "Yum Yum" sauce you can go back to the "What's for Dinner" section under Hibachi Stir Fry and make the sauce, however, I suggest that you do this before you start your rice.

This will allow the flavors to marry together.

FARRO BURRITO BOWL

SERVINGS: 4 | PREP: 15 MINS | TOTAL: 25 MINS

INGREDIENTS

3 Tab extra-virgin olive oil

2 Tab chopped fresh cilantro

2 Tab fresh lime juice

2 tsp honey

¾ tsp ancho chile powder

¾ tsp kosher salt

½ tsp black pepper

2 cups cooked farro

½ cup red bell peppers, coarsely chopped

¼ cup red onions, coarsely chopped

½ cup green bell peppers, coarsely chopped

½ cup yellow squash, coarsely chopped

½ cup zucchini, coarsely chopped

1 (15-oz.) can unsalted black beans, rinsed and drained

½ cup cojita cheese, crumbled

1 medium avocado, sliced

Cilantro, rough chopped (garnish)

Lime wedges

DIRECTIONS

1. In a medium-size bowl add the first seven ingredients except for 1 tablespoon of olive oil. Whisk together and set aside. Reserve 1 1/2 tablespoons cilantro mixture. In a large skillet over medium-high heat, add the remaining olive oil and sauté the vegetables for 5-7 mins until al dente; remove from heat, and set aside.

2. Add cooked farro to the cilantro vinaigrette mixtures. Divide farro mixture, chopped sautéed vegetables, beans, cheese, and avocado among 4 shallow bowls. Drizzle with reserved 1 1/2 tablespoons cilantro mixture. Serve with lime wedges and cilantro.

CHEF NOTES

The plant-based brand is entirely up to you; the most popular are Beyond Meat and Impossible. You can also use frozen patties or black bean burgers; the taste and texture will be different; however, differences are not deficient.

Also, you can replace the mayo with a vegan-based mayo that will make your burger dairy-free; this is true for the cheese as well.

VEGETARIAN DOUBLE STACK

SERVINGS: 2 | PREP: 10 MINS | TOTAL: 25 MINS

INGREDIENTS

1 lb plant-based meat, refrigerated and ground

2 tsp onion powder

2 tsp garlic powder

1 tsp paprika

1 tsp kosher salt

1 tsp black pepper

2 Tab olive oil

1 8 count sesame seed buns

1 cup iceberg, chopped

4 slices American cheese

1 Tab white onion, minced

6 dill pickle slices

SECRET SAUCE

½ cup mayonnaise

1 Tab ketchup

1 Tab mustard

4 tsp sweet pickle relish

2 tsp white onion, finely minced

1 tsp white vinegar

1 tsp granulated sugar

1/8 tsp salt

DIRECTIONS

FOR SECRET SAUCE: Mix all the ingredients in a small bowl. Cover and refrigerate for an hour, at least, before serving.

FOR THE BIG MACS: In a medium-sized mixing bowl add ground plant-based meat, onion, garlic powder, salt, and pepper. Mix all together and form 4 4oz patties and set aside.

2. Lightly toast four bottom buns and set them aside. In a medium-sized skillet, cook the patties for 3-5 minutes on each side, or until cooked through.

3. On the first of the two bottom buns, add ½ tablespoon of the Special Sauce, ½ teaspoon of the onion, ⅛ cup of shredded lettuce, cheese, and one hamburger patty.

4. Place the other bottom bun on top, and top it with the same items mentioned above, but no cheese. Top with the remaining bun top.

CHEF NOTES

The plant-based brand is entirely up to you; the most popular are Beyond Meat and Impossible. You can also use frozen patties or black bean burgers; the taste and texture will be different; however, differences are not deficient.

Also, you can replace the mayo with a vegan-based mayo that will make your burger dairy-free; this is true for the cheese as well.

SPICY JAMBALAYA

SERVINGS: 6-8 | PREP: 10 MINS | TOTAL: 40 MINS

INGREDIENTS

2 Tab Olive oil

1 Tab Cajun seasoning

1 medium yellow onion, diced

1 medium bell pepper, stemmed, seeded, and chopped

3 celery stalks, chopped

3 garlic cloves, chopped

½ small jalapeno, seeded and minced

1 large tomato, diced

1 16 oz can crush tomatoes

2 bay leaves

1 tsp smoked paprika

1 tsp dried thyme

1 cup uncooked long-grain rice

3 cups vegetable broth, warm

1 can kidney beans, drained and rinsed (optional)

Salt and pepper to taste

DIRECTIONS

1. Place a large, heavy-bottomed pot over medium-high heat and add the oil. After it gets hot, add the onion, bell pepper, Cajun seasoning, and celery, then cook for about 5 minutes, until they become translucent but not brown.

2. Add the garlic, jalapeno, tomatoes, crushed tomatoes, bay leaves, paprika, and thyme. Let everything cook until some of the tomato juice releases, about 1 minute.

3. Add the rice and slowly pour in the broth. Lower the heat to medium and let the dish cook until the rice absorbs all the liquid, 20 to 25 minutes. If you're using kidney beans, put them in to cook with the rice after 15 minutes have passed.

4. Taste and adjust the salt, and pepper if needed.

RAINBOW SPRING ROLLS

SERVINGS: 8 | PREP: 30 MINS | TOTAL: 30 MINS

INGREDIENTS

8 to 10 (10-inch) rice paper wrappers

4 green leaf lettuce leaves, torn into large pieces

1 cup fresh basil leaves

¼ cup chopped fresh cilantro leaves

½ cup matchstick carrots

½ cup shredded purple cabbage

1 red bell pepper, thinly sliced

4 ounces vermicelli or rice noodles (the thinner the better)

½ English cucumber, seeded and cut into long matchsticks

Kosher salt and freshly ground black pepper, to taste

FOR PEANUT SAUCE

¼ cup all-natural creamy peanut butter

4 teaspoons reduced-sodium soy sauce

1 tablespoon freshly squeezed lime juice

2 teaspoons brown sugar

2 teaspoon chili garlic sauce

1 teaspoon freshly grated ginger

DIRECTIONS

1. To make the peanut sauce, whisk together peanut butter, soy sauce, lime juice, brown sugar, chili garlic sauce, and ginger in a small bowl. Whisk in 2-3 tablespoons water until desired consistency is reached; set aside. Prepare rice noodles in boiling water for about 10 minutes (read instructions on package), then drain and set aside.

2. To assemble spring rolls, pour hot water into a shallow dish or skillet and immerse rice paper to soften for about 10-15 seconds. Transfer to a damp cutting board or a damp towel and gently spread out edges into a circle. It may take a little practice, so do not feel bad if your first few attempts are a fail!

3. Place lettuce, basil, and cilantro in the center of each wrapper; top with carrots, cabbage, bell pepper, cucumber, and rice noodles; season with salt and pepper to taste.

4. Bring the bottom edge of the wrap tightly over the filling and then fold in the sides, rolling from bottom to top until the top of the sheet is reached, being careful not to tear the rice paper; cover with damp paper towels. Repeat with remaining wrappers and filling.

5. Serve immediately with peanut sauce.

CHEF NOTES

You can also replace the rice noodles with avocado if you want to limit the amount of carb consumption. Sweet Chili sauce is another great dipping sauce that compliments the spring rolls.

KALE QUINOA & APPLE SALAD

SERVINGS: 6 | PREP: 10 MINS | TOTAL: 30 MINS

INGREDIENTS

½ cup tricolor dry quinoa

6 cups slightly packed chopped kale, ribs removed

2 gala apples, cored and chopped

½ cup pumpkin seeds, toasted

¼ cup red bell pepper, small diced

½ cup dried cranberries

4 oz goat cheese or feta, crumbled

DRESSING

Zest of 1 large lemon

2 1/2 tbsp lemon juice

3 tbsp extra virgin olive oil

1 tsp Dijon mustard

½ tsp chili flakes

1 garlic clove, minced

1 tsp honey

1/2 tsp each salt and pepper

DIRECTIONS

1. Cook quinoa according to directions on the package and cool completely. While quinoa is cooling, whisk together olive oil, lemon juice, honey, Dijon, and salt in a jar or bowl.

2. Pour ¾ dressing over kale, chill: Add kale to a salad bowl, whisk dressing once more, then pour ¾ of the dressing over kale and toss until kale is evenly coated. Cover bowl and chill for 15 minutes (adding the dressing and letting it rest helps soften kale a bit).

3. Remove salad from refrigerator, add apples, quinoa, pumpkin seeds, and cranberries. Pour remaining dressing over salad, then toss. Add goat cheese and toss just lightly. Serve or store covered in the refrigerator for up to 4 hours.

CURRY CAULIFLOWER & ROASTED BUTTERNUT SQUASH
CILANTRO LIME VINAIGRETTE
SERVINGS: 4 | PREP: 15 MINS | TOTAL: 45 MINS

INGREDIENTS

1 head cauliflower, cut into medium-sized florets

2-3 cups butternut squash, cut into ½ inch cubes

1 tablespoon olive oil

1 teaspoon curry powder

½ teaspoon ground turmeric

½ teaspoon garlic powder

¼ teaspoon red cayenne pepper

Freshly ground salt and pepper

2/3 cup thawed frozen peas (optional)

¼ cup diced green onion

1/3 cup dried dates

½ cup finely chopped cilantro

CILANTRO LIME VINAIGRETTE

1 huge bunch of fresh cilantro

½ cup avocado oil

2 tablespoons of rice wine vinegar

1 clove garlic

1 teaspoon kosher salt

½ teaspoon red pepper flakes

¼ cup water, if needed

DIRECTIONS

1. **FOR THE DRESSING**: Blend all the ingredients for about one minute until smooth. Add the water if you need more volume in the blender to make the consistency smooth. Set aside.

2. Preheat oven to 350 degrees F. In a large bowl, put cauliflower florets and cubed butternut squash drizzle olive oil, then curry powder, turmeric, garlic powder, red cayenne pepper, and season with salt and pepper. Use clean hands to toss everything together until it's well coated with oil and spices. Spread out evenly on a baking sheet lined with parchment paper. Roast for 30 minutes, flipping halfway in between. Squash should be fork-tender but still have a slight bite.

3. Once done cooking, add roasted squash and cauliflower to a medium bowl. Add in the thawed peas, green onion, dates, and cilantro. Fold the dressing into the rest of the ingredients until they are well coated. Garnish with a few extra scallions, dates, and cilantro.

CHEF NOTES

This recipe can be served hot or cold. Perfect for leftovers or made a day in advance. The flavors penetrate more if you make a day in advance!

ULTIMATE VEGETARIAN LASAGNA

SERVINGS: 6-8 | PREP: 20 MINS | TOTAL: 1 HOUR

INGREDIENTS

2 tablespoons extra-virgin olive oil

2 large carrots, chopped

1 red bell pepper, chopped

1 medium zucchini, chopped

1 medium yellow onion, chopped

1 cup eggplant, chopped

1 cup mushrooms, chopped (I used baby Bella)

3 cloves garlic, minced

½ teaspoon dried oregano

1 (24-ounce) marinara-style pasta sauce of choice

¼ teaspoon salt

5 oz baby spinach

1 cup ricotta cheese

Freshly ground black pepper, to taste

½ cup grated Parmesan

9 lasagna noodles, cooked

2 Tab fresh basil, chopped

2 cups freshly shredded low-moisture, part-skim mozzarella cheese

DIRECTIONS

1. Preheat the oven to 425 degrees. In a large skillet over medium heat, warm the olive oil and add the carrots, bell pepper, zucchini, yellow onion, eggplant, mushrooms, and salt. Cook, stirring every couple of minutes, until the veggies are golden on the edges, about 8 to 12 minutes.

2. Add a few large handfuls of spinach. Cook, frequently stirring, until the spinach has wilted. Repeat with remaining spinach and cook until all the spinach has wilted, about 3 minutes. Remove the skillet from the heat and set aside. Add the minced garlic, next ½ teaspoon kosher salt, basil, and oregano. Cook for another 2 minutes. Remove the pan from the heat. Add the marinara pasta sauce and stir to combine. In a medium-size mixing bowl, mix ricotta, Parmesan, and cracked pepper.

3. Take half of your vegetable marinara, put it in a food processor, and pulse for 30 seconds to a minute. Spread ½ cup pulse tomato sauce evenly over the bottom of a 9" by 9" baking dish and put the remainder of the pulse sauce back into the pot with vegetable marinara. Layer 3 lasagna noodles on top (snap off their ends to fit, and/or overlap their edges as necessary). Spread half of the ricotta mixture evenly over the noodles. Top with ¾ cup tomato sauce, then sprinkle ½ cup shredded cheese on top.

4. Top with 3 more noodles, followed by the remaining ricotta cheese mixture; sprinkle ½ cup shredded cheese on top, then spread ¾ cup tomato sauce over the top, then sprinkle ½ cup shredded cheese on top. Repeat the process until noodles, sauce, and remaining cheese are finished.

5. Line a baking sheet with parchment paper or foil just in case the sauce boils over. Bake for 25 to 30 minutes until the cheese is melted, hot and bubbly, and the top is spotty brown. Let rest 5 to 10 minutes, then serve.

SWEET POTATO KALE & QUINOA CAKE
MANGO SALAS

SERVINGS: 4-6 CAKES | PREP: 10 MINS | TOTAL: 20 MINS

INGREDIENTS

1 medium sweet potato (about 6 oz), chopped (skin on)

¼ cup, finely chopped kale

½ shallot, diced

½ tsp salt

½ tsp pepper

2 garlic cloves, minced

1 Tab ginger, minced

2 tsp olive oil

1 Tab coconut oil

½ cup cooked quinoa

2 Tab fresh basil, chopped

MANGO SALSA

2 ripe mangoes, peeled, pitted, and small dice

1 small red onion, peeled and diced

1-2 jalapenos, seeded and diced

1/2 cup chopped fresh cilantro, loosely packed

juice of one lime

salt and pepper

DIRECTIONS

1. For the mango salsa, toss all ingredients together until combined. Season with salt and pepper if needed and refrigerate. Heat a large skillet over medium-low heat and add 1/2 tablespoons olive oil. Add in sweet potato, kale, shallots, ginger, 1/4 teaspoon of salt, and 1/4 teaspoon of pepper, stir, cover, and cook for 10-12 minutes, or until potato is soft. Remove lid and add garlic, cooking for 30 seconds.

2. Transfer potato mixture to a large bowl, then slightly mashing potato with a fork and add quinoa, herbs, remaining salt, and pepper and mix well. Using your hands to bring it together, form four equally sized patties. Heat the same skillet over medium heat and add coconut oil. Add cakes and cook for 3-4 minutes per side, or until golden brown. Serve with mango salsa!

NEXT

THE SWEET SPOT

AT HOME WITH
Chef Mark Phillips

THE SWEET SPOT

Ok, I must be honest; I am not a sweets person! However, I love to bake, create, and make beautiful edible treats. Bread and pasta are my weakness, but like most things, "everything in moderation." Baking is one of the things we most commonly hear people say they cannot do. Unless you are allergic to sugar at some point in your life, you have indulged in some form of dessert goodness. With the popularity of cupcakes, custards, pies, tarts, cakes, ice cream, and so much more, I wanted to give you some of my favorite dessert recipes that I enjoy making for my clients, friends, and family.

We have all heard the saying, "You cannot have your cake and eat it too!" Ummmm... why not? The word "dessert" originated from the French word desservir, meaning "to clear the table." Hence why, dessert usually comes at the end of your meal. Although I may not eat a lot of desserts, it is something about taking that first bite of whatever you have just baked or decorated. I will make a whole caramel fudge snickers brownie cheesecake and only eat one slice to get my fix and give the rest away. Don't worry; that recipe and many more are in the pages to follow!

If you do not know anything about food, one thing you must know: baking is a science. One cannot be so free-flowing with the ingredients when it comes to baking, as the results may not be the most presentable and/or palatable. There are six essential tips that I wanted to share with you that generally apply to baking as a whole. The first tip is to "**READ THE RECIPE BEFORE STARTING**". Read the recipe from beginning to end until you understand all the steps, for example, so you don't forget to separate your eggs if needed or over mixing, and your cake could not come out fluffy. It is also important to have your "mise en place" (a French culinary phrase that means "putting in place") this way; you won't be stuck with rock-solid butter when it should be softened.

KNOWING YOUR OVEN IS CRITICAL! Every oven is different and will do different things to your food at different times. Two of the most common myths are that ovens will distribute heat unevenly or the temperature gauge will be inaccurate. Hot spots are natural, and ovens sometimes lie. For example, if your cookies come out of the oven with the back-right side looking burnt and the front-left looking doughy, you will have to start rotating your pan halfway through. Most ovens have a digital or manual knob temperature gauge to tell you what your general oven temperature is. If you don't get a burst of heat at the beginning, bread, cakes, and cream puffs won't rise. If the heat is too low for too long, they could dry out. Rack placement is also important. Depending on how your oven circulates heat and where the heating element is, there is a big difference between baking on the top, middle, or bottom rack.

IS THERE A FUNDAMENTAL DIFFERENCE BETWEEN BAKING SODA AND BAKING POWDER, YES!

Baking works because of a series of chemical reactions. It also means that you need the right chemicals to make the right things happen at the right time. Baking powder and baking soda have a lot in common. They're both types of chemical leaveners, meaning they generate gas during the mixing and baking of a batter or dough that "raises" the baked good. Cakes, muffins, biscuits, quick breads, and anything you are baking that doesn't include yeast rely on these compounds to produce a light texture or "crumb."

USING THE RIGHT FLOUR.

There are various types of flour, and each one serves its purpose; and with some, you can use it in place of another while, on the other hand, it will be a disaster. Flours, ranging from whole-wheat to pastry, to corn, to almond, cake, and back to all-purpose. Flour is ground wheat berries that come right off the stalk. Whole-wheat flour is the whole-wheat berry, whereas white flour is made from the inside of the berry, called the endosperm. The two proteins in flour, gliadin and glutenin, are what make gluten when made wet. Gluten is a protein! Bread flour is so named because it has higher protein levels giving you more lift, structure, and air pockets in your bread. Cake flour is a much softer, lower-protein flour and gives your delicate baked goods a tender crumb. As the name suggests, all-purpose flour is somewhere in the middle and very versatile. Self-rising flour has baking powder and salt already mixed in.

WHOLE EGGS, EGG WHITES, AND EGG YOLK.

Eggs are one of the main ingredients in a lot of baking, and the purpose of eggs in baking is they create structure and stability within a batter, they help thicken and emulsify sauces and custards, they add moisture to cakes and other baked goods, and can even act as glue or glaze. The egg white is almost exclusively protein and water, whereas the yolk is made up of different proteins, fat, and vitamins. The contents of an egg-white allow it to whip up into a foam, using the protein to build structures. On the other hand, an egg yolk is a creamy emulsifier that adds richness and thickness.

KNOWING THE DIFFERENCE BETWEEN OILS AND BUTTER.

Let's start with butter; you will notice in the recipes to follow that butter either needs to be cold or room temperature. Trust me, whether it is cookies or pie crust, the temperature makes a difference, and the outcome will let you know. Cold butter, like in pie crust, is used to create flaky layers. As the butter melts in the oven, it keeps the dough from binding together, which creates flakiness. Room-temperature butter is almost always creamed with sugar, which creates little air pockets. As a rule of thumb, anywhere you see melted butter in a recipe, you can substitute oil; if you see cold or room temperature, the final product won't come out right if you try to use oil instead of butter.

I hope these tips give you a better insight into baking or a refresher for those who are already experienced. The most important thing to remember is to have fun and try not to let cooking and baking intimidate you. Like always, get your grocery list together, grab an apron, and let's get to the sweet spot.

CARAMEL & FUDGE SNICKERS BROWNIE CHEESECAKE

SERVINGS: 8-10 | PREP: 20 MINS | TOTAL: 1 HOUR 15 MINS

INGREDIENTS

FOR THE CRUST

1 ½ graham cracker crumbs

3 Tab sugar

7 Tab butter, melted

FOR THE CHEESECAKE

16 oz cream cheese, room temperature

16oz sour cream

2 tsp vanilla extract

3 large Eggs

2 tsp corn starch

¾ cup sugar

TOPPINGS

1 box brownie mix (I used Ghirardelli), baked and cubed

2 snickers bars, frozen

¼ cup caramel topping

¼ cup chocolate fudge topping

DIRECTIONS

1. Preheat oven to 350 degrees. Prepare graham cracker crust first by combining graham cracker crumbs, sugar and stirring well. Add melted butter and use a fork to combine ingredients well. Pour crumbs into a 9" Springform pan and press firmly into the bottom and up the sides of your pan. Set aside.

2. Make the filling by mixing the room-temperature cream cheese and sugar until smooth. Mix in the eggs one at a time (about 10-15 seconds), then add vanilla, mixing until smooth. To avoid beating too much air into the batter, use a mixer set at low-medium speed. To avoid lumps, make sure the cream cheese is softened and/or at room temperature.

3. Add sour cream and corn starch, and stir until well-combined. If using a stand mixer, make sure you pause periodically to scrape the sides and bottom of the bowl with a spatula so that all ingredients are evenly incorporated.

4. Pour cheesecake batter into prepared springform pan. To ensure against leaks, place the pan on a cookie sheet that has been lined with foil. Transfer to the center rack of your oven and bake for about 55-60 minutes. Edges will likely have slightly puffed and may have just begun to turn a light golden brown, and the center should spring back.

5. Remove the cheesecake from the oven and set it on a rack to cool. Once the cake is cool, refrigerate and cover for at least 2 hours. Just at the tail end of the two hours, remove the snickers from the freezer and place them in a large ziplock bag. Use a cutting board and mallet and break up the snickers into pieces, set aside. Take two tablespoons of caramel and fudge, drizzle it over the cheesecake, and next top with pre-cooked cubed brownie pieces. Drizzle the remaining fudge and caramel over the brownie and sprinkle the crushed snickers evenly. You can serve immediately or refrigerate until ready to serve.

CHEF NOTES

Please see my Salted Caramel Brownie recipe if you want to use homemade brownies instead of boxed ones. To make cutting easier, you can pre-slice the cheesecake before you add the brownie and snickers; however, that is entirely up to you.

FOR OREO CRUST

26 classic Oreo cookies
4 Tab butter, melted.

1. Place Oreo cookies in the food processor (do not remove the cream filling) and pulverize until only fine crumbs remain. If you do not have a food processor, place cookies in a Ziploc bag (let all the air out before sealing) and beat with a rolling pin or mallet until only fine crumbs remain.

2. In a separate, medium-sized microwave-safe bowl, heat butter until completely melted.

3. Pour cookie crumbs into the melted butter and stir until well combined.

4. Pour cookie crumbs into the prepared pan and use your hands and/or the clean bottom of a glass or measuring cup to tamp crumbs tightly into the bottom and sides of your pan.

RED VELVET CUPCAKES VANILLA BEAN CREAM CHEESE

SERVINGS: 12-15 CUPCAKES | PREP: 30 MINS | TOTAL: 25 MINS

INGREDIENTS

2 2/3 cups plain cake flour

4 tbsp cocoa powder, unsweetened

1 tsp baking soda

Pinch of salt

½ cup unsalted butter softened

1 ½ cups white sugar

2 eggs, at room temperature

1 cup vegetable oil

1 tsp white vinegar

2 tsp vanilla extract

1 cup buttermilk, at room temperature

3 Tab red food coloring liquid

1 pack cupcake paper cups

FROSTING

14 oz Cream Cheese, room temperature

½ cup unsalted butter softened

1 ½ tsp Madagascar vanilla bean extract

4 cups powdered sugar, sifted

DIRECTIONS

1. Preheat oven to 350 degrees. Line a non-stick 12-Cup muffin pan with cupcake paper cups or butter 2 2 x 21cm / 8" round cake pans (sides and base) and dust with cocoa powder. Sift the dry ingredients and whisk to combine in a bowl.

2. Place butter and sugar in a bowl and beat with an electric beater or in a stand mixer until smooth and well combined. Add eggs, one at a time, beating in between to incorporate. At first, it will look curdled - keep beating until it's smooth. Add vegetable oil, vinegar, vanilla, buttermilk, and red food coloring. Beat until combined.

3. Add dry ingredients and beat until just combined. Divide batter evenly amongst cupcake pans or if using cake pans, divide between cake pans. Bake for 25 - 30 minutes on the same shelf or until a toothpick inserted into the center comes out clean. Rest for 10 minutes in the pan, then turn out onto a cooling rack and allow to cool.

4. **FROSTING**: Beat cream cheese, butter, and vanilla together for 3 minutes. Add powder sugar and beat for 2 more minutes or until the frosting is light and fluffy. If your frosting is too runny just add more powder sugar.

5. Transfer to a piping bag. Pipe a large dollop of cream cheese frosting on each cupcake and spread it to your heart's desire.

HOMEMADE CHOCOLATE CHIP COOKIE ICE-CREAM SANDWICHES

SERVINGS: 10 SANDWICHES | PREP: 20 MINS | TOTAL: 45 MINS

INGREDIENTS

2 cups all-purpose flour

1 tsp baking soda

½ tsp kosher salt

1 cup butter, barely melted but NOT hot

¾ cup light brown sugar, packed

2/3 cup granulated sugar

2 tsp vanilla extract

1 tsp apple cider vinegar

1 large egg

2 cups semisweet chocolate chips

4 cups or ½ gallon of your favorite ice-cream (I used vanilla bean ice cream)

Chocolate Chips

DIRECTIONS

1. Preheat oven to 350 degrees. Line a baking sheet with parchment paper, and set aside. In a medium-size bowl mix together the flour, baking soda, and sea salt; set aside.

2. In a large bowl, beat butter, sugar, vanilla extract, and vinegar until smooth; slowly beat in the egg until just combined.

3. Mix the flour mixture into the wet just until combined; stir in chips. Use a large cookie or ice-cream scoop (about 2 tablespoons in size), and drop about 3 inches apart onto the prepared cookie sheet.

4. Bake for 8 to 10 minutes; they will be light brown around the edges and will look undone in the center, but that is ok. If you like a crispier cookie, add 3-5 minutes to your baking time. Allow to sit on the sheet for 10 minutes before moving to a rack to cool.

5. Take one cookie and place a scoop of ice cream (about 1/4 cup) on the flat side of the cookie. Top with the flat side of the second cookie to make a sandwich. Serve immediately or wrap tightly in plastic wrap and freeze.

OPTIONAL: Place mini chocolate chips in a bowl or on a plate. Roll the sides of the sandwich in the chips.

MINI SUGAR COOKIE FRUIT TARTS

SERVINGS: 24 | PREP: 20 MINS | TOTAL: 40 MINS

INGREDIENTS

2 ¼ cup all-purpose flour

1 ¼ cup sugar

½ tsp baking powder

½ tsp baking soda

¼ tsp salt

2 tsp vanilla extract

1 cup butter, room temperature

1 egg

Extra sugar for dipping

CREAM CHEESE FILLING

1 8 oz package cream cheese, room temperature

½ cup powdered sugar

1 cup heavy cream

½ tsp vanilla

Fresh fruit (I used raspberries, blueberries, kiwi, and strawberry)

DIRECTIONS

1. Preheat oven to 350 degrees. Coat mini cupcake pan with baking spray. In a large bowl with a standing or hand mixer, cream butter and sugar together until light and fluffy, about 1 minute.

2. Add in the egg and vanilla extract until combined. Add in flour, baking soda, baking powder, and salt. Mix until just combined, making sure you scrape down the sides of the bowls now and then.

3. Roll dough into 1-inch balls and then roll in sugar.

4. Place in mini-cupcake pan, using the back of a ½ tsp, and make a small indention. Bake for 8-10 minutes or until the edges are golden. Allow cooling before removing it from the pan.

FOR THE FILLING: Cream together the cream cheese and powdered sugar until thick and smooth. Add heavy cream and vanilla extract. Pipe or spread the filling into the cooled cookie shells. Top with fresh fruit. Store in the fridge until ready to serve.

LEMON ZEST SOUR CREAM DONUTS

SERVINGS: 10 DONUTS | PREP: 15 MINS | TOTAL: 2 HOURS

INGREDIENTS

FOR THE DONUTS

1 ¼ cup cake flour

1 cup all-purpose flour

1 ½ teaspoons baking powder

1 teaspoon salt

¼ teaspoon ground nutmeg

½ cup sugar

2 tablespoons salted butter, at room temperature

2 large egg yolks

½ cup sour cream

Canola oil, for frying

FOR THE GLAZE

3 cups powdered sugar, sifted

1 teaspoon corn syrup

¼ teaspoon salt

½ teaspoon vanilla extract

¼ lemon zest

¼ cup hot water

DIRECTIONS

1. In a bowl, sift together the cake & all-purpose flour, baking powder, salt, and nutmeg. In the bowl of a stand mixer fitted with a paddle attachment, beat the butter and sugar together until sandy. Add the egg yolks and mix until light and thick. Add the dry ingredients to the mixing bowl in 3 additions, alternating with the sour cream, ending with the flour mixture. The dough will be sticky. Cover with plastic wrap and chill for 1 hour.

2. On a floured surface, roll out the dough to about ½ inch thickness. Use a doughnut cutter, or I used a biscuit cutter and a tall two-ounce shot glass to cut, dipping the cutters into flour as necessary to prevent sticking. You should get about 10 doughnuts and holes.

3. Pour 2 inches of canola oil into a heavy-bottomed pot with a deep-fry thermometer (if not a deep-fry thermometer, put the heat on medium to medium-high: test donut holes to desired golden brown). Heat to 325°F. Fry the doughnuts a few at a time, being careful not to overcrowd the pot. Fry on each side for about 2 minutes, be careful not to let them burn. Let drain on a paper bag to soak up the excess grease.

FOR THE GLAZE: Mix all ingredients in a bowl with a whisk until smooth. Immerse each doughnut into the glaze. Place on a wire rack above a sheet pan to catch any excess glaze or on parchment paper if you do not have a wire rack. Let sit for 20 minutes until the glaze is set. Doughnuts are best served the day they are made but maybe stored in an airtight container at room temperature for a few days.

EASY CHOCOLATE MOUSSE CAKE

SERVINGS: 8 | PREP: 5 MINS | TOTAL: 18 MINS

INGREDIENTS

8 ounces semi-sweet chocolate chips

1 cup butter

1 tsp vanilla extract

2 cup powdered sugar

4 eggs

4 egg yolks

12 Tab flour

Fresh berries (optional garnish)

DIRECTIONS

1. Preheat oven to 425 degrees. Spray 8 ramekins cups with non-stick cooking spray (preferably baking non-stick cooking spray) and place on a baking sheet.

2. In a microwave-safe bowl, melt butter and chocolate until butter is melted. Stir until chocolate is melted. Stir in sugar until well blended. Whisk in vanilla extract, eggs, and egg yolks. Stir in flour. Divide evenly between baking dishes.

3. Bake 13-15 minutes until sides are firm and center is soft. Let stand 1 minute before removing. Top with berries. Serve warm with ice cream or my favorite gelato.

SWEET POTATO CHEESECAKE

SERVINGS: 8-10 | PREP: 20 MINS | TOTAL: 1 HOUR 15 MINS

INGREDIENTS

FOR THE CRUST

1 ½ graham cracker crumbs

3 Tab sugar

7 Tab butter, melted

FOR THE CHEESECAKE

16 oz cream cheese, room temperature

½ cup sugar

½ light brown sugar, packed

1 medium-size sweet potato, baked and smashed

1 Tab cinnamon

½ tsp nutmeg

½ tsp all-spice

16oz sour cream

2 tsp vanilla extract

3 large Eggs

DIRECTIONS

1. Preheat oven to 350 degrees. Prepare graham cracker crust first by combining graham cracker crumbs, sugar, and stirring well. Add melted butter and use a fork to combine ingredients well.

2. Pour crumbs into a 9" Springform pan and press firmly into the bottom and up the sides of your pan. Set aside.

3. Make the filling by mixing the room-temperature cream cheese, sweet potato, sugar, cinnamon, nutmeg, and all-spice until smooth. To avoid beating too much air into the batter, use a mixer set at low-medium speed. Mix in the eggs one at a time (about 10-15 seconds), then add vanilla, again mixing until smooth. To avoid lumps, make sure the cream cheese is softened and/or at room temperature.

4. Add sour cream and corn starch, and stir until well-combined. If using a stand mixer, make sure you pause periodically to scrape the sides and bottom of the bowl with a spatula so that all ingredients are evenly incorporated.

5. Pour cheesecake batter into prepared springform pan. To ensure against leaks, place the pan on a cookie sheet that has been lined with foil. Transfer to the center rack of your oven and bake for about 55-60 minutes. Edges will likely have slightly puffed and may have just begun to turn a light golden brown, and the center should spring back.

6. Remove the cheesecake from the oven and set it on a rack to cool. Once the cake is cool, refrigerate and cover for at least 2 hours.

STRAWBERRY & MASCARPONE PUFFY PASTRY WITH CRUSHED PISTACHIOS

SERVINGS: 6-8 | PREP: 10 MINS | TOTAL: 30 MINS

INGREDIENTS

1 sheet of puff pastry, thawed

1 egg, whisked

2 lbs strawberries, stemmed and quartered

¾ cup granulated sugar

1 tsp orange zest

8 oz mascarpone

8 oz of whipped cream

½ teaspoon vanilla

WHIPPED CREAM

1 cup heavy whipping cream

1 tsp vanilla extract

1 Tab sugars, powdered

1/4 cup crushed pistachios

CHEF NOTES

If you do not want to make the whipped cream from scratch, you can buy premade whipped cream from the grocery store!

DIRECTIONS

1. Preheat oven to 400 degrees. On a parchment-lined baking sheet, roll out the puff pastry dough to a large rectangle.

2. In a small bowl, whisk together the egg and the water. Use a knife to score a border ¾ of an inch inside from the edge of the puff pastry. Use a fork to pierce the inside of the tart several times. Brush the pastry with the egg wash along the border. Sprinkle with sugar if desired.

3. For the whipped cream: In a large bowl, whip cream until stiff peaks are just about to form. Beat in vanilla and sugar until peaks form. Make sure not to over-beat; cream will then become lumpy and butter-like.

4. Bake for 20 minutes until golden brown and cooked. Set aside to cool. While the puff pastry is cooking, gently combine strawberries, the orange zest, and ¼ cup granulated sugar in a large bowl so that the strawberries are coated with sugar. Let sit to macerate for 20 minutes. Prepare the topping in a large bowl; stir together the whipped cream, ½ cup white sugar, and mascarpone cheese.

5. After the strawberries have been macerated for 30 minutes, place a sieve over a bowl and drain the liquid out of the strawberry mixture into the bowl. Take that strawberry liquid and put it in a small saucepan. Add a tablespoon of balsamic vinegar to the saucepan and bring to a boil on medium-high heat.

6. Boil until the liquid has reduced to the consistency of syrup, remove from heat, and let cool.

7. Once the puff pastry is cool, spread the mascarpone mixture over the bottom of the tart shell and then the strawberries. Keep refrigerated until ready to slice and serve. Just before serving sprinkle desired amount of pistachios on-top of each slice.

SALTED CARAMEL BROWNIES

SERVINGS: 10 | PREP: 10 MINS | TOTAL: 45 MINS

INGREDIENTS

1 ½ cup all-purpose flour

1/3 cup cocoa powder

½ tsp salt

½ cup semi-sweet chocolate chips

1 cup butter

4 oz semi-sweet chocolate

2 cups sugar

4 eggs

Coarse sea salt

CARAMEL SAUCE

1/2 cup sugar

4 tablespoons salted butter

3 tablespoons heavy cream

pinch of salt

DIRECTIONS

1. Preheat oven to 350 degrees. Lightly grease a 9x9 baking dish. Melt together the butter and semi-sweet chocolate, and let cool slightly.

2. Stir in the sugar and eggs. Sift together flour, cocoa powder, and salt, then add to the sugar and eggs along with the 4oz chocolate chips.

3. Spread the batter in the prepared baking dish and bake for 30-35 minutes.

CARAMEL SAUCE: While the brownie is baking, place the sugar in a small saucepan over medium-high heat. Stir frequently; the sugar will form clumps and eventually become smooth. Remove from heat. Add butter and stir in. Add cream and stir in. Return to heat, and let it get smooth and bubbly for another few minutes. Set aside.

To check the doneness of the brownie, insert a toothpick, and see if it comes out mostly clean. Let cool completely before topping with caramel sauce and sprinkle with sea salt.

DEEP DISH APPLE PIE

SERVINGS: 12 | PREP: 25 MINS | TOTAL: 1 HOUR

INGREDIENTS

FOR THE CRUST

3 ¾ cups all-purpose flour, more for dusting surfaces

1 ½ teaspoon kosher salt

½ teaspoon sugar

3 sticks (12 oz) cold unsalted butter, cut into large dice

Ice water

FOR THE FILLING

10 cups apples, thin peeled and sliced (I used granny smith)

½ cup granulated sugar

½ cup brown sugar, firmly packed

¼ cup all-purpose flour

2 tsp ground cinnamon

½ tsp nutmeg

½ tsp all-spice

1 tsp lemon juice, fresh

2 Tab butter, cubed

DIRECTIONS

1. For the crust: Make the crust: In a food processor or stand mixer, mix the flour, salt, and sugar. Add butter and pulse (or mix at medium-low speed) until the pieces are coated with flour. Add 1/2 cup ice water (no ice) and mix until incorporated. Keep dribbling in ice water, a tablespoon at a time, mixing until the dough just comes together into a lump. It should be moist but not sticky. Turn out onto a lightly floured surface. (If the dough feels wet, use a little extra flour.) Press the dough together, turning over a few times, until smooth and solid.

2. Shape into 2 disks, using a rolling, about 1/3 of the dough for the top crust and the remaining 2/3 for the bottom crust. Wrap separately in plastic wrap and refrigerate for at least 1 hour and up to 2 days.

3. On a lightly floured surface or non-stick baking mat, roll out the larger disk to about ¼-inch thickness. The size and shape will depend on your dish. Use the crust to line a large 2 ½- to 3-quart baking dish, like a 10-inch round or 9-inch square, at least 2 inches deep. Refrigerate while you prepare the apples.

4. Preheat oven to 425 degrees. In a large bowl, toss apples with sugar, flour, cinnamon, nutmeg, and all-spice. Place the bottom crust in your pan. Fill with apples, mounded slightly. Cover with a latticework crust.

5. Bake 15 minutes in the preheated oven. Reduce the temperature to 350 degrees. Continue baking for 35 to 45 minutes, until apples are soft.

MINI BLUEBERRY & LEMON BUNDT CAKES

SERVINGS: 8 | PREP: 25 MINS | TOTAL: 50 MINS

INGREDIENTS

2 ½ cups all-purpose flour

2 tsp baking powder

½ tsp salt

1 cup unsalted butter, room temperature

1 ¾ cups granulated sugar

Finely grated zest of 2 large lemons

3 large eggs at room temperature

1 tsp vanilla extract

¾ cup buttermilk

1 ¼ cups fresh blueberries

FOR THE GLAZE

1 ¾ cups confectioners' sugar

¼ cup lemon juice

1 zest of one lemon

1 tsp salted butter, melted

DIRECTIONS

1. Preheat the oven to 350°F. With butter and flour, grease each mini bundt pan well. You can also use a 10-cup Bundt pan.

2. In a medium bowl, whisk together flour, salt, baking powder, and baking soda. In a liquid measuring cup, whisk together the buttermilk, vanilla, and lemon juice.

3. In a large bowl or stand mixer bowl, combine the butter, sugar, and lemon zest with an electric mixer on medium speed for about 4 minutes or until light and fluffy. Beat in the eggs and egg yolk one at a time until combined.

4. Beat in 1/3 of the flour mixture, followed by half of the buttermilk. Repeat with half of the remaining flour and remaining buttermilk. Finish by folding in the remaining flour until just incorporated. Fold in the blueberries. Fill each mini bundt pan about 2/3 of the way full. You may need to bake in two batches, depending on your pan.

5. Bake for about 25-30 minutes, or until a wooden skewer inserted into the center comes out clean. If you're using a regular bundt pan, bake for 45-50 minutes. Let cakes cool for 20 minutes in the pan, and then flip onto a wire rack to cool completely.

FOR THE GLAZE: In a small bowl, mix confectioners' sugar, lemon juice, and melted butter until smooth. Drizzle over the top of the cake and let it roll down the sides.

IRISH CREAM CRÈME BRULEE

SERVINGS: 6 | PREP: 15 MINS | TOTAL: 1 HOUR 15 MINS

INGREDIENTS

2 cups heavy cream

1/3 cup white sugar

6 egg yolks

½ cup Irish cream liqueur (I used baileys)

1/8 tsp kosher salt

1 tsp. vanilla extract

superfine sugar, for topping

DIRECTIONS

1. Preheat oven to 300 degrees. Place 6 ramekins on a towel set in a roasting pan at least 3 inches deep.

2. In a medium saucepan, combine cream and salt. Cook over low heat until hot. Remove from heat and add vanilla extract.

3. In a medium-size bowl, beat yolks, sugar, and Irish cream until eggs turn light yellow.

4. Add about a ¼ cup of the cream to the eggs. Continue to add the cream slowly, so the temperatures gradually integrate. Pour into ramekins. Fill the baking dish with hot boiling water halfway up the sides of the dishes. Bake for 30-40 minutes or until set. Remove from oven and cool completely. Once cooled, place in the refrigerator for at least a couple of hours (overnight is even better!).

5. Unwrap the custards and sprinkle about 1 teaspoon of superfine sugar onto each. Gently shake the custards so the sugar coats the entire top surface, then tip the custards to a 45-degree angle and shake off excess sugar.

6. Using a small hand torch, melt the sugar by making short passes over the top of the custards with the flame not quite touching. Continue melting the sugar until it turns deep brown. Once the sugar has dissolved and turned to caramel, the cold custard underneath will harden the sugar into a crispy crust. Serve immediately.

ANGEL FOOD MIXED BERRY SHORT CAKE

SERVINGS: 10-12 | PREP: 25 MINS | TOTAL: 1 HOUR

INGREDIENTS

1 ¾ cups granulated sugar

1 cup cake flour, sifted

¼ tsp salt

12 large egg whites, at room temperature

1 ½ tsp cream of tartar

1 ½ tsp pure vanilla extract

¼ tsp almond extract (optional)

WHIPPED TOPPING

2 cups heavy whipping cream

2 tsp vanilla extract

2 Tab sugars, powdered

2 cups strawberries, steamed and 1 cup quartered

1 cup blueberries

1 cup raspberries

¼ cup granulated

DIRECTIONS

1. **FOR THE CAKE**: Preheat the oven to 350 degrees and place the oven rack in the lowest position. Sift ½ cup sugar and flour together twice; set aside. Add cream of tartar, extracts, and salt to egg whites; beat on medium speed until soft peaks form. Gradually add remaining sugar, about 2 tablespoons at a time, beating on high until stiff peaks form. Gradually fold in flour mixture, about ½ cup at a time.

2. Gently spoon into an ungreased 10-in. tube pan. Cut through batter with a knife to remove air pockets. Bake until lightly browned and the entire top appears dry, 35-40 minutes. Immediately invert pan; cool completely, about 1 hour. Run a knife around the side and center tube of the pan. Remove cake to a serving plate.

3. While the cake is baking, gently combine 1 cup quartered strawberries, ½ blueberries, ½ raspberries, and ¼ cup granulated sugar in a large bowl so that the berries are coated with sugar. Let sit to macerate for 20 minutes.

4. **FOR THE WHIPPED CREAM**: In a large bowl, whip cream until stiff peaks are just about to form. Beat in vanilla and sugar until peaks form. Make sure not to over-beat; cream will then become lumpy and butter-like.

5. Once cool, slice in half and layer with half of the whipped cream and macerated berries. Top with remaining half, whipped cream, and non-macerated berries. Slice, serve, and enjoy!

CINNAMON BUNS

SERVINGS: 12 | PREP: 25 MINS | TOTAL: 2 HOURS

INGREDIENTS

2 ¼ tsp active dry yeast or instant yeast

1 cup milk lukewarm

½ cup granulated sugar

1/3 cup butter unsalted, softened, or margarine

1 tsp salt

2 eggs

4 cups all-purpose flour

FILLING

½ cup melted butter, plus more for the pan

½ cup sugar, plus more for the pan

½ cup dark brown sugar, packed

2 Tab ground cinnamon

ICING

8 ounces cream cheese, room temperature

1/3 cup salted butter, softened

2 cups powdered sugar

½ Tab vanilla extract

DIRECTIONS

1. Heat oven to 350 degrees F.

2. In a small bowl, dissolve yeast in warm milk and set aside. Mix milk, sugar, melted butter, salt, and egg in a large bowl. Add 2 cups of flour and mix until smooth. Add yeast mixture. Mix in remaining flour until dough is easy to handle. Knead dough on a lightly floured surface for 5 to 10 minutes. Place in a well-greased bowl, cover, and let rise until doubled in size, usually 1 to 1 ½ hour.

3. When doubled in size, punch down dough. Roll out on a floured surface into a 15 by 9-inch rectangle. Spread melted butter all over the dough. Mix sugar and cinnamon and sprinkle over buttered dough. Beginning at the 15-inch side, roll up the dough and pinch the edge together to seal. Cut into 12 to 15 slices.

4. Coat the bottom of a baking pan with butter and sprinkle with sugar. Place cinnamon roll slices close together in the pan and let rise until dough is doubled, about 45 minutes—Bake for about 30 minutes or until nicely browned.

5. Meanwhile, while the rolls are baking, make the icing by mixing all the icing ingredients and beat well with an electric mixer until fluffy and smooth. Spread over slightly cooled rolls.

NEXT

IT'S 5 O'CLOCK SOMEWHERE.

AT HOME WITH
Chef Mark Phillips

IT'S 5 O'CLOCK SOMEWHERE.

Who does not enjoy a good cocktail or a glass of wine! My mother may not want to hear this, but I definitely had my first drink before age 21 (not advocating underage drinking). Still, it was not until my late twenties and early thirties that I began to appreciate the craft of creating a cocktail. During that time, I also built an appreciation for wine and the various varietals; my personal favorite is sauvignon blanc or cabernet sauvignon. The front of the house (FOH) and back of the house (BOH) can not work without one another, so I began to seek out cocktails made by a mixologist. Food was exchanged for drinks, the cooks would make something special for the bartenders, and the bartenders would pour heavy for the cooks. They create drinks using fresh ingredients, herbs, fruits, spices, and even eggs. Don't worry; I will not get too intricate with the cocktails but rather introduce new flavors to your already existing spirits.

But first, I wanted to start by giving you a simple wine crash course and spirit guide. Wine is an alcoholic beverage made with the fermented juice of grapes. Often, people ask me, "What wine pairs with food?" You can technically drink any wine (or cocktail) you want; however, certain wines lend themselves to the protein, dessert, or cheese. The notes in the wine can either enhance the flavor profile or compete, which you do not want. With this information, I hope you become more comfortable trying new wines or gaining better knowledge as you go out into the world.

Wine comes from all over the world; some of the oldest countries that have been producing wine are Italy, Spain, and France, but wine has expanded internationally for several years. There are over 1,300 wine grape varieties; however, only about 100 make up the world's consumption. They include light sweet white wines like Moscato and Riesling to deep dark red wines like Syrah and Cabernet Sauvignon. Let us start by covering the 9 major styles of wine.

THERE ARE 9 STYLES OF WINE:

- Sparkling Wine
- Light-Bodied White Wine
- Full-Bodied White Wine
- Aromatic (sweet) White Wine
- Rosé Wine
- Light-Bodied Red Wine
- Medium-Bodied Red Wine
- Full-Bodied Red Wine
- Dessert Wine

With each wine, I wanted to provide you with taste, description, style, and food pairings. Now let's go through the 8 most popular wines. Each wine listed below also includes alternative varieties that taste similar. So, if you prefer wine, you might also like its alternatives.

Cabernet Sauvignon

TASTE: Black Cherry, Black Currant, Baking Spices, and Cedar

STYLE: Full-Bodied Red Wine

DESCRIPTION: Cabernet Sauvignon is a full-bodied red grape first heavily planted in the Bordeaux region. Today, it's the most popular wine variety in the world!

Wines are full-bodied with bold tannins (tannin in wine adds both bitterness and astringency, as well as complexity) and a long persistent finish driven mainly by the higher levels of alcohol and tannin often accompany these wines.

FOOD PAIRING: lamb, beef, smoked meats, burgers, portabella mushrooms, firm cheeses like aged cheddar, and hard cheeses like Pecorino.

ALTERNATIVES: Merlot, Cabernet Franc, or Bordeaux blend

Syrah

TASTE: Blueberry, plum, tobacco, cured meat, black pepper, violet

STYLE: Full-Bodied Red Wine

DESCRIPTION: Syrah (aka Shiraz) is a full-bodied red wine that's heavily planted in the Rhône Valley in France and Australia. Syrah is commonly blended with Grenache and Mourvèdre to create the red Rhône blend. The wines have intense fruit flavors and medium-weight tannins. The wine often has a meaty (beef broth, jerky) quality.

FOOD PAIRING: lamb, beef, smoked meats, pork, American and French firm cheeses like white cheddar, and hard cheeses like Spanish Manchego.

ALTERNATIVES: Malbec.

Zinfandel

TASTE: A broad, exotic array of fruits from stone nectarine, to red raspberry or sour cherry, to blue blueberry, to black blackberry, Asian 5 Spice Powder, Sweet Tobacco

STYLE: Medium-bodied to full-bodied Red Wine

DESCRIPTION: Zinfandel is a medium-bodied red wine that originated in Croatia. Zinfandel is a red grape that may be better known in its pink variation, White Zinfandel. Wines are fruit-forward and spicy with a medium-length finish.

FOOD PAIRING: chicken, pork, cured meat, lamb, beef, barbecue, Italian, American, Chinese, Thai, Indian, full-flavored like cheddar, and firm cheeses such as Manchego.

ALTERNATIVES: Grenache

Pinot Noir

TASTE: Very red fruited cherry or cranberry and red-floral, often with appealing vegetal notes of beet, rhubarb, or mushroom.

STYLE: Lighter-bodied Red Wine

DESCRIPTION: Pinot Noir is a dry, light-bodied red that was first widely planted in France. The wines typically have higher acidity and a soft, smooth, low tannin finish.

FOOD PAIRING: chicken, pork, veal, duck, cured meat, French, German, cream sauces, soft cheeses, nutty medium-firm cheeses like Gruyère.

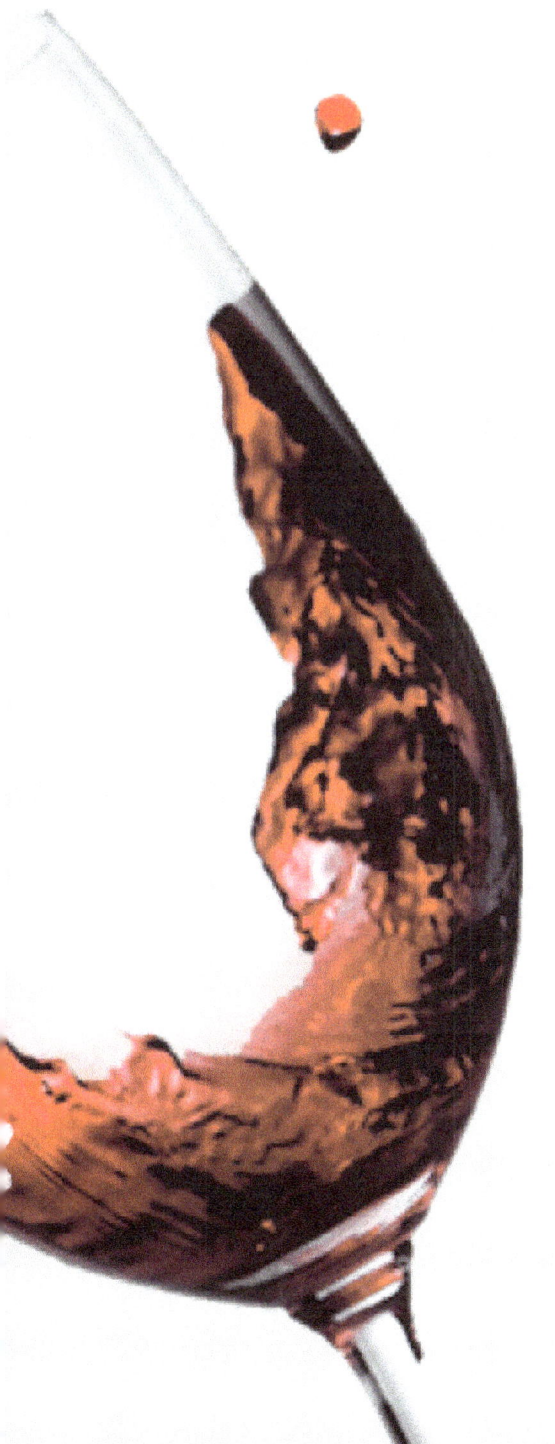

Chardonnay

TASTE: Yellow citrus Meyer lemon, yellow fruits like pear and apple, tropical fruits such as banana and pineapple, and often a touch of butterscotch, vanilla, or toasted caramel notes from the oak. Sometimes depending on the brand, butter notes appear.

STYLE: Medium- to Full-Bodied White Wine

DESCRIPTION: Chardonnay is a dry, full-bodied white wine that was planted in large quantities for the first time in France. When oak-aged, Chardonnay will have spicy, bourbon-y notes. Unoaked wines are lighter and zesty with apple and citrus flavors. Chardonnay is the white grape of Burgundy.

FOOD PAIRING: lobster, crab, shrimp, chicken, pork, mushroom, French, cream sauces, soft cheeses such as triple cream brie, medium-firm cheeses like Gruyère.

Sauvignon Blanc

TASTE: Aggressively citrus driven like grapefruit, with some exotic fruits such as honeydew melon, passion fruit, kiwi, and always a surprising quality of mint and green pepper.

STYLE: Light- to Medium-Bodied White Wine

DESCRIPTION: Sauvignon Blanc is a dry white grape first widely planted in France. Wines are tart with herbal, green, or citrus fruit flavors.

FOOD PAIRING: fish, chicken, pork, veal, Mexican, Vietnamese, French, herb-crusted goat cheese, nutty cheeses such as Gruyère.

Pinot Gris

TASTE: ADelicate citrus hints of lime and orange zest and fruits like apples and pear, white floral notes, and cheese rind

STYLE: Light-Bodied White Wine

DESCRIPTION: Pinot Gris is a dry light-bodied white grape planted heavily in Italy and France and Germany. Wines are light to middle-weight and easy to drink, often with some bitter flavor on the palate.

FOOD PAIRING: Salad, delicate poached fish, chicken, light, and mild cheeses.

Riesling

TASTE: Citrus and stone fruit such as white peach or nectarine always feature prominently, although there are also usually floral and sweet herbal elements as well.

STYLE: Floral and fruit-driven aromatic white that comes in variable sweetness. Some producers choose not to ferment all the grape sugar and therefore make the wine in an "off-dry" style

DESCRIPTION: Always highly high in acid, when made as a table wine, Rieslings can be harmoniously sweet or dry. The wine is subjective because some people find dry styles too acidic and sweet styles too sentimental, but the sweetness is always a winemaking decision and not inherent to the grape.

FOOD PAIRING: chicken, pork, duck, turkey, cured meat, Indian, Thai, Vietnamese, Moroccan, German, washed-rind cheeses and fondue.

ALTERNATIVES: Moscato or Gewürztraminer

Glassware

You can drink wine from whatever vessel you choose, be it a wine glass, coffee mug, mason jar, or dixie cup. You can ditch the glass altogether and drink straight from the bottle for all I care (been there, done that). However, different styles of wine glasses were made for a reason, which is to enhance the drinking experience. To keep it simple, you at least should have a standard red wine, white wine, and champagne glass(es). Now, on the other hand, when it comes to cocktails, you will see in some of the recipes that I have to choose specific glasses.

WINE GLASSES

Red Wine Glass

White Wine Glass

Sparkling Wine Glass

Dessert Wine Glass

COCKTAIL GLASSES

Highball Glass

Coupe Glass or Classic Champagne Glass

Rocks Glass

Martini Glass

Shot Glasses

Cocktail

If you've ever been to a fancy cocktail bar or your favorite cheers, the thought of recreating those drinks at home may seem like a daunting undertaking. Making cocktails at home is not as hard as it seems, and it can be incredibly fun (and delicious). Bartenders have an array of dramatic and unique tools that exist only for making cocktails and a seemingly comprehensive knowledge of how to blend them. I have compiled this guide of essential cocktail tools to help dispel any confusion and to get you on the right path to making tasty libations. These days you can find kits with most of the items I have listed below built into one easy-to-carry package for the at-home bartender. You will see me referring to some of these tools in the recipes in this chapter.

JIGGER

Or, as my friend Vanessa would say, "that little devil thing". The first tool needed, of course, is a way to measure liquid. In this case, a jigger. Seasoned bartenders can pour without a measure, but many still elect to, as accuracy is important in making cocktails. The slightest imbalance can throw the whole drink off. I prefer not to use one, but I would recommend it for even balance.

SHAKER

There are many varieties of shakers out there, some with built-in strainers; if not, grab a glass that fits. This is required for any drink that needs to be shaken, and the glass half can also be used as a mixing glass.

STRAINER

If your shaker did not come with a strainer, I recommend getting one. After drinks are shaken with ice in the shaker, they need to be strained into their final vessel.

BAR SPOON

Once you have the technique down, stirring a drink is immensely satisfying. Granted, you can use a regular spoon; however, this particular spoon has an extended handle that makes it easy to stir.

MUDDLER

A muddler is a bartender's tool, used like a pestle to mash—or muddle—fruits, herbs, and spices in the bottom of a glass to release their flavor.

JUICER

A juicer, also known as a juice extractor, is a tool used to extract juice from fruits, herbs, leafy greens, and other vegetables in a process called juicing. It crushes, grinds, and/or squeezes the juice out of the pulp.

BITTERS

Bitters are made by infusing a neutral spirit with various aromatics, including spices, tree bark, roots, seeds, fruits, etc. Bitters were initially developed and marketed for medicinal purposes, with ingredients generally thought to impart good health preserved in a neutral liquor.

SIMPLE SYRUP

If you can boil water, you can make a simple syrup. The staple cocktail sweetener more than earns its name, consisting, simply, of equal-parts granulated sugar and water. From there, the variations are endless.

TOOL GUIDE

The 6 Basic Spirits

Before we get to the different types of liquor, you must understand the differences between the main terms. Distillation takes the process one step further. Distillation turns fermented beverages into much more robust versions of themselves by separating the alcohol from the water. The alcohol in the liquid becomes much more concentrated by removing the water.

So first things first, liquor is a distilled alcoholic beverage, and it is made by distilling anything that's been fermented. If you don't know what fermentation or distillation is, that probably sounds like nonsense to you.

There is no doubt about it;

the liquor world can be highly confusing to the uninitiated. There are many distilled spirits available today, though just six base liquors form the foundation of most cocktails and liqueurs. Brandy, gin, rum, tequila, vodka, and whiskey are each unique and have distinct styles within themselves.

So, like the wine, I wanted to give you some basic keynotes on each of the 6 spirits. What it is distilled from, the flavor profile, the different styles, and the overall cocktail profile of the spirit:

Brandy

DISTILLED FROM: Fruit. Primarily grapes, though apple, apricot, cherry, peach, and other fruits are also used.

FLAVOR PROFILE: Fruity burnt wine.

STYLES: Cognac, Armagnac, Spanish Brandy, Pisco, American Brandy, Grappa, Eau-de-vie, Flavored Brandies

COCKTAIL PROFILE: Brandy was used in several classic cocktails and tends to be used in more sophisticated drinks that include just a few ingredients. Many modern brandy recipes are breaking this mold, however, and experimenting with brandy in some very unique flavor combinations.

Gin

DISTILLED FROM: Neutral grains such as barley, corn, rye, and wheat. Flavored with a variety of botanicals, which vary by brand.

FLAVOR PROFILE: Herbal, dry. The primary flavor that defines gin comes from juniper berries, thus the 'piney' aroma and taste.

STYLES: London Dry Gin, Plymouth Gin, Old Tom Gin, Genever, New American Gin

COCKTAIL PROFILE: Gin's dry profile makes it a perfect candidate for dry (non-sweet) cocktails, including many classics and martinis. It is a nice base for cocktails with just a few ingredients and pairs well with some of the lighter fruits, and, naturally, works well with herbs.

Rum

DISTILLED FROM: Sugar. Either molasses or pure sugar cane.

FLAVOR PROFILE: Sweet. Toasted sugar. Varies by style and region.

STYLES: Light Rum, Gold Rum, Dark Rum, Over-Proof Rum, Spiced Rum, Cachaca, Flavored Rum

COCKTAIL PROFILE: Rum's sweeter flavor makes it one of the more versatile spirits. It is the obvious base for tropical drinks. On the other side of the spectrum, it also appears in several warm cocktails. It was one of the first liquors to be mixed into drinks, so there are some nice classic rum cocktails to choose from.

Tequila

DISTILLED FROM: Agave.

FLAVOR PROFILE: Vegetal, earthy with semi-sweet and spicy tones.

STYLES: Blanco, Reposado, Anejo, Extra-Anejo, Gold (Other agave spirits are mezcal, pulque, sotol, raicila, and baconara, but these are not tequilas.)

COCKTAIL PROFILE: Tequila has an excellent flavor profile for mixing into a variety of cocktails. It also makes a perfect base for spicy cocktails and is very popular for party shots. There are margaritas and frozen cocktails in which tequila is mixed with any fruit imaginable.

Vodka

DISTILLED FROM: Neutral grain (rye, corn, wheat, etc.) or potato. Some are distilled from beets, grapes, and other bases. Vodka can be the 'catch-all' category for white spirits that fit nowhere else.

FLAVOR PROFILE: Neutral alcohol/ethanol. It varies greatly depending on the base and added flavorings. Distinguished more by texture: oily vs. medicinal.

STYLES: Clear vodka is typically distinguished by the base it was distilled from and/or the region it was produced. Flavored vodkas are a popular category

COCKTAIL PROFILE: Vodka's neutral taste makes it the most versatile spirit available today. Vodka cocktails can be found on almost every imaginable flavor profile, from sweet to savory, fruits to herbs and spices. Martinis and shooters are popular vodka drinks as well.

Whiskey

DISTILLED FROM: Malted grains, which vary by style. It can include a mixture of corn, rye, wheat, barley, etc.

FLAVOR PROFILE: Roasted, malted grain with oak undertones. There are distinct characteristics in each style.

STYLES: Irish Whiskey, Scotch, Bourbon, Rye Whiskey, Tennessee Whiskey, Canadian Whisky, Blended Whiskey, Flavored Whiskey, and other emerging types based on location (e.g., Japanese Whisky)

COCKTAIL PROFILE: Whiskey is another of the more versatile cocktail bases available, and with so many styles, there is the opportunity for great diversity in flavor profiles. It mixes well with other liquors to create complex drinks and pairs well with several fruits, particularly the darker fruits. Warm drinks are also immensely popular with whiskey.

Now that you have some knowledge on wines and spirits, it's time to get to the cocktail recipes. You will see recipes ranging from sangrias (wine-based) to an old fashion (spirit based). These cocktails are my takes on some of the classics, each with a different flare and fresh ingredients and meant to complement the individual spirit. Some of these drinks are seasonal as fruits may not be available year-round. I enjoy a good cocktail, a crisp glass of white wine, or a full-body red wine; regardless of your preference, the most important thing is to drink responsibly and not to drink a drive. Cheers!!!

WHITE WINE SANGRIA

SERVINGS: 6 | PREP: 10 MINS | TOTAL: 10 MINS

INGREDIENTS

1 cup strawberries, halved

1 cup pineapple, cubed

1 peach, sliced

¼ cup granulated sugar

1 apple, sliced

1 orange, sliced

1 lime, sliced

1 750ml bottle white wine, chilled

1 cup seltzer water

½ cup vodka (optional)

DIRECTIONS

1. In a medium bowl, combine strawberries, pineapple, peach, sugar, and vodka. Refrigerate for 1 hour.

2. To a large pitcher, add refrigerated fruit and apple, orange, and lime slices. Pour in white wine and seltzer and stir to combine. Serve well chilled.

JALAPENO PALOMA

SERVINGS: 1 COCKTAIL | PREP: 5 MINS | TOTAL: 5 MINS

INGREDIENTS

1 oz Lime juice, fresh

2 oz Grapefruit juice, fresh

1 tsp Agave

1 thin slice Jalapeno Crushed

1 ½ oz Silver Tequila

Handful of Ice

Grapefruit slice for garnish

DIRECTIONS

1. Rim the glass with lime juice and salt. Add the jalapeño slices to a glass, squeeze the lime wedge into the glass, and muddle the jalapeño slices in the lime juice.

2. Add ice to the glass, then pour in the tequila and grapefruit juice into the glass, stir to combine. Garnish with jalapeño slices.

CHEF NOTES

Can you have this drink without tequila? Yes, you can! You may want to add a touch of club soda or lemon-lime soda to give the drink a bit more body, but that is up to you. Simply omit the tequila and enjoy.

CBD BLACKBERRY MULE

SERVINGS: 2 COCKTAILS | PREP: 5 MINS | TOTAL: 5 MINS

INGREDIENTS

½ cup blackberries, fresh

2 Tab lime juice, fresh

4 oz vodka

3 cups ginger beer

1/3 oz Cbd simple syrup (optional see chef notes)

Fresh mint leaves, garnish

DIRECTIONS

In a cocktail shaker, combine the blackberries, lime juice, and CBD simple syrup and muddle. Add the vodka and stir. Strain the mixture evenly between 2 chilled copper mugs and add the ginger beer (1.5 cups each). Top with ice and garnish with mint leaves, lime wedges, and/or a few fresh blackberries. Serve immediately!

CHEF NOTES

If you do not want the effects of CBD, replace it with regular simple syrup. For the CBD simple syrup:

1. Bring ½ cup water to boil in a small saucepan and add ½ cup sugar until dissolved.

2. Add 2g (grams) ground decarboxylated dried cannabis flower.

3. Cover and reduce for 30 mins, then remove from heat and let cool.

4. Strain through cheesecloth into a jar and can store for up to one month.

This cocktail is good for hangovers or a relaxing night at home.

CUCUMBER GIMLET

SERVINGS: 4 | PREP: 5 MINS | TOTAL: 5 MINS

INGREDIENTS

8 oz gin

2 limes, quartered

1 cup cucumber, cut into 1-inch pieces

4-6 basil leaves, fresh and rough chopped

2 oz simple syrup

1 cup ice

DIRECTIONS

1. Combine lime, cucumber, and basil leaves in a shaker or medium size jar and muddle thoroughly. Add gin, simple syrup, and ice, then place the top onto the shaker and shake vigorously for 5 to 10 seconds. Strain and serve up or over ice or a single ice cube.

2. Garnish with a lime and cucumber slice.

RASPBERRY LEMONADE MIMOSA

SERVINGS: 4 | PREP: 5 MINS | TOTAL: 5 MINS

INGREDIENTS

8 oz chilled Brut Champagne

4 oz raspberry lemonade, pulp strained out if desired

1-pint raspberry sorbet

Fresh raspberries

DIRECTIONS

1. Place one small scoop of sorbet into a champagne flute. Pour about 2 ounces of Champagne into a champagne flute (about 2/3 of the way up)

2. Pour about 1 ounce of raspberry lemonade into the flute (almost filling the flute).

3. Top with fresh sugared raspberries. Enjoy!

MINT JULEP

SERVINGS: 2 | PREP: 5 MINS | TOTAL: 5 MINS

INGREDIENTS

4-5 fresh mint leaves, - roughly torn

1 ½ simple syrup

crushed ice

splash of cold water (optional)

2 oz bourbon

spring of fresh mint (garnish)

DIRECTIONS

1. To the bottom of the serving glass, add mint leaves and simple syrup. Muddle together with a muddler or handle of a wooden spoon. Top with plenty of crushed ice, then pour in a splash of cold water and bourbon.

2. Stir, garnish with the sprig of mint, and serve!

CHEF NOTES

If you want to make the mint julep with a fruity twist, add strawberries and ginger ale. If so, you will need one cup (fresh or frozen). In a blender, pulse together the strawberries and ginger ale just a few times to break up the strawberries. Then you would add the strawberry mixture to the bottom of the glass; follow the remainder of the steps after you add the ice.

To make this a nonalcoholic version, remove bourbon.

SPICY BLOODY MARY

SERVINGS: 1 | PREP: 7 MINS | TOTAL: 7 MINS

INGREDIENTS

1 cup ice cubes

1 ½ ounce vodka

3/4 cup spicy tomato-vegetable juice

2 dashes Worcestershire sauce

1 dash hot pepper sauce

1 pinch salt and pepper to taste

Lemon juice

1 stalk celery

2 stuffed green olive

DIRECTIONS

In an 11-ounce highball glass, stir together tomato juice, vodka, Worcestershire sauce, hot sauce, salt, and pepper. Fill the glass with ice, then pour the mixture into the second glass. Pour back and forth 3 to 4 times to mix well, then sprinkle lemon juice over. Garnish with a celery stalk and lemon wedge (if using) and serve.

CHEF NOTES

For added spice, increase the hot sauce or add 1-2 teaspoons horseradish.

RED WINE SANGRIA

SERVINGS: 6 | PREP: 10 MINS | TOTAL: 10 MINS

INGREDIENTS

2 apples, diced into chunks

1 orange, rind removed and diced into chunks

1 lime, sliced into rings

2 tablespoons lemon juice

1 750ml bottle medium-bodied red wine

¼ cup brandy

1 Tab sugar

½ cup orange juice

sparkling water, to serve *optional*

DIRECTIONS

1. Pour the wine into a pitcher, then add the lemon juice, lime, and orange wedges into the wine. Toss in the fruit wedges (try to remove seeds first, if possible) and add the orange juice, sugar, and brandy, stirring gently until the sugar dissolves. Cover the pitcher with plastic wrap and chill it in the refrigerator for 4 to 8 hours or overnight to marry the fruit and wine flavors.

2. When ready to serve, give the sangria one last stir and pour over a glass of ice. Top with sparkling water for some bubbles if desired.

CHEF NOTES

The fruit variation is entirely up to you.

Some people like more of a berry-forward sangria by adding in blackberries, blueberries, and/or strawberries. The key is allowing all the flavors to come together by letting the sangria marry for several hours. Also, depending on the type of wine, you selected you may want to adjust the sugar content, add or reduce.

CADILLAC MARGARITA

SERVINGS: 2 | PREP: 5 MINS | TOTAL: 5 MINS

INGREDIENTS

4 ounces reposado tequila

1 oz Cointreau

1 oz Grand Marnier

½ orange

½ lime

ice

salt

DIRECTIONS

1. Roll out orange and lime on a sturdy surface to release the juice. Slice in half, reserving ½ of each for the second round or another recipe.

2. If desired, salt the rim of the serving glass (old fashioned or rocks glass) then fill with ice. In a cocktail shaker juice, the orange and lime. Add in the tequila, Cointreau, and Grand Marnier.

3. Fill the shaker with ice, cover and shake to combine, then strain into the serving glass.

ROSEMARY OLD FASHION

SERVINGS: 2 | PREP: 5 MINS | TOTAL: 5 MINS

INGREDIENTS

4 oz rye whiskey (or regular)

½ oz rosemary syrup

4 dashes orange bitters

Orange peel for garnish

2 springs of rosemary (plus more for garnish)

DIRECTIONS

1. To make the rosemary syrup, combine equal parts water and sugar in a pot. Add several sprigs of fresh rosemary. Heat mixture until just barely simmering and remove from heat. Let the syrup steep for 10 minutes, and then remove the rosemary.

2. In a rock glass combines the whiskey, rosemary syrup, and orange bitters. Add ice and stir to chill the drink. Garnish with rosemary spring and orange peel.

PENICILLIN

SERVINGS: 1 | PREP: 5 MINS | TOTAL: 5 MINS

INGREDIENTS

2 oz Blended scotch

3/4 oz Fresh lemon juice

3/4 oz honey-ginger syrup*

1/4 oz Islay single-malt scotch

Garnish: Candied ginger

DIRECTIONS

Combine the blended scotch, lemon juice, and syrup in a cocktail shaker and shake with ice. Strain over fresh ice into an old-fashioned or rocks glass. Top with the single-malt scotch and garnish with skewered, candied ginger.

HONEY-GINGER SYRUP: Combine 1 cup honey, 1 6-inch piece of peeled and thinly sliced ginger, and 1 cup water in a saucepan over high heat and bring to a boil. Reduce heat to medium, and simmer 5 minutes. Place in the refrigerator to steep overnight. Strain with cheesecloth or strainer.

THE FRENCH CONNECTION

SERVINGS: 2 | PREP: 5 MINS | TOTAL: 5 MINS

INGREDIENTS

2 oz Hennessy

1 oz Grand Marnier

2 large ice ball

Lime juice

DIRECTIONS

Split the spirit ingredients evenly between two old-fashioned/rocks glasses. Dash each of the glasses with lime juice, add ice ball, stir gently, and enjoy.

CHEF NOTES

This drink is also good in shot format; place all ingredients in a shaker and strain in shot glasses.

FRENCH 75

SERVINGS: 1 | PREP: 4 MINS | TOTAL: 4 MINS

INGREDIENTS

2 ounces gin

¾ ounce fresh lemon juice

½ ounce simple syrup

2 ounces Champagne

Long spiral lemon twist (for serving)

DIRECTIONS

Add all the ingredients except the Champagne into a shaker with ice and shake well. Strain into a Champagne flute. Top with the Champagne and garnish with a lemon twist.

CHEF NOTES

This drink is also good with cognac; switch out the gin.

CLASSIC DIRTY MARTINI

SERVINGS: 1 | PREP: 5 MINS | TOTAL: 5 MINS

INGREDIENTS

2 oz gin

½ oz dry white vermouth

½ oz olive juice

Blue cheese olives

DIRECTIONS

Add all the ingredients into a shaker or mixing glass with ice and stir. Strain into a chilled martini glass. Garnish with 2 to 4 blue cheese olives, skewered.

ACKNOWLEDGMENTS

In between getting back to work life during a pandemic and writing this cookbook, it has taken a village to complete this cookbook! This cookbook has been a labor of love, and I didn't want this book just another one sitting on the shelf. I wanted to share my love of cooking and a portion of my life story with the world. I also wanted to provide some culinary education and foods I eat and cook for friends and family.

To my wonderful Mother, Gwen Hamlin, thank you for always being there for me and supporting me on my ever-evolving journey. I appreciate your encouraging my dreams and being my cheerleader in life. I love you!

To my Aunt Pat, thank you for constantly showering me with love and support; the way you love our family is something that I cherish; you and my mother constitute a significant impact on why I love cooking and how it brings us all together. To my uncle Joe, through your daily living and farming, you showed me how to care for food in a way like no other. Taking the time to grow vegetables, raise chickens, and can his food has made food a necessity and a passion (rest in peace).

To my father, Steven M. Phillips, Sr., thank you for your love and support; I miss you very much, and may you continue to rest in peace. To my grandmother, Sylvia Phillips, you have always told me how proud I make you and that you love me unconditionally. To my family (the Friends and Phillips), thank you for believing in me, being a driving force for me to continue to strive for more, and reminding me that I have my village by my side; I love you all, and thank you very much! Thank you for your impact on my life; I love you very much.

To my bonus sister, Erica Smith (and your husband Karey Smith and daughter Kenzie), thank you for opening your home up to me during a necessary time in my life. I cannot thank you enough for your love, the push to stretch myself further in my talent, and for being a great chosen family member overall.

To my uncle, Kevin Phillips, and friend Keya Grant, thank you both for opening your homes to me for the photoshoot and for your love and support. To Cristina Neculcea, thank you for shooting the pictures in the Appetizer & Snack section. Thank you to Paul Biagui and Lindsay Cloer for the cover and lifestyle shoots.

To Donna Knutson for story editing, Jose Tavares for recipe editing, and Ben for formatting; thank you all! To my lawyer, Shay Lawson, thank you for your guidance and direction and for being a good friend. To Jaaz Jones, thank you for writing my foreword and all you do for me!

Thanks to all my wonderful family, friends, and clients for your excitement, enthusiasm, and honest opinions! Thank you for your continued support, and I look forward to many more libations and culinary creations! Thank you to the readers and anyone who takes the time to invest in my culinary journey and send me positive vibes. Thank you to all the chefs and culinary creators who inspire and challenge me to stretch in my craft.

Most of all, thank you, God, universe, all-mighty, or whatever name you call the spiritual existence that lives in all of us! Without that internal and external guidance, I do not know where I would be; THANK YOU, GOD!

INDEX

WHERE DO I START

Kitchen Essentials 16

Knives 19

Cookware & Bakeware 23

Basic Kitchen Conversions & Equivalents 25

Metric to U.S. Cooking Conversions 26

U.S. to Metric Cooking Conversions 27

Basic Kitchen Knife Cuts 28

Kitchen Terminology 30

Cooking Internal Temperature Chart 34

SOUPS, SALADS & SANDWICHES

Crab & Corn Chowder 38

Chicken Toscana 40

Herb Chicken Noodle 43

Sage Roasted Butternut Squash Soup 44

Kale & Quinoa Greek Salad 47

Asian-Style Chicken Chopped Salad 48

Arugula, Mozzarella & Tortellini Salad 51

Rosemary Fried Chicken & Avocado Cobb Salad 52

Watermelon, Feta & Mint Salad 55

Fried Shrimp Po'boy 57

Grilled Portabella Mushroom Caprese Panini 59

Jibarito "Plantain" Sandwich 60

Lobster Rolls 63

Herb de Provence Chicken Salad Croissant Sandwich 64

Basil Pesto 65

Grilled Lamb or Chicken Pita Wraps.. 66

APPETIZERS & SNACKS

Smoked Salmon Cream Cheese & Dill Crostini... 74

Pimento Cheese Deviled Eggs.. 77

Peach & Burrata Bruschetta... 78

Brown Sugar Jerk Grilled Wings... 81

Kale & Cremini Turkey Meatballs.. 82

Chicken or Beef Satay... 85

Crab Stuffed Mushrooms... 86

Bacon Wrapped Shrimp.. 89

Chicken Taquitos w/ Cilantro Lime Cream... 90

Spinach Tortellini & Mozzarella Caprese Skewers... 93

Crispy Goat Cheese Poppers w/ Hot Honey... 94

Shrimp & Guacamole Wonton Cups.. 97

Vegetable Spring Rolls.. 98

Roasted Red Pepper & Garlic Hummus.. 100

Roasted Corn Salsa... 101

Spinach & Artichoke Dip... 102

COMING FROM WHERE I'M FROM

Rosemary Garlic Biscuits & Gravy.. 111

Fried Green Tomatoes & Remoulade Sauce... 113

Blackened Shrimp & Grits... 114

Baked Macaroni & Cheese... 117

Jalapeno Cheddar Corn Bread... 118

Dusted Ranch Fried Chicken Wings... 121

New Orleans Inspired Gumbo.. 122

My "Momma's" Potato Salad.. 125

Southern Collard Greens.. 126

Not-So Traditional Chicken Pot Pie"..................................... 124

BBQ Pork Spare Ribs... 131

Georgia Peach Cobbler... 132

Banana Pudding... 135

Braised Oxtails... 136

WHAT IS FOR DINNER?

Grilled Rosemary Peppercorn Lamb Chops......................... 146

Shrimp Scampi... 149

Herb de Provence Roasted Chicken..................................... 150

Street Taco Tuesday 3 Ways... 152

Red Wine Braised Short Ribs... 157

Salmon Florentine 158

Cajun Pork Tenderloin.. 161

Fajita Loaded Baked Potato... 162

Naan Flatbread Pizzas... 165

Green Chili Chicken Enchiladas 166

Hibachi Fried Rice... 169

The Ultimate Crab Boil 170

Pan-seared Halibut.. 173

Grilled Chicken Bruschetta.. 174

Italian Stuffed Shells... 175

EAT YOUR VEGETABLES

Gouda Cauliflower Macaroni & Cheese............................... 181

Thai Coconut Curry Vegetables & Noodles....................... 182

Roasted Red Pepper Hummus Wrap 185

Mushroom Bolognese Pasta 186

Greek Barley Bowl 189

Baked Sweet Potato Broccoli Pesto 190

Cauliflower Fried Rice 193

Farro Burrito Bowl 194

Vegetarian Double Stack 197

Spicy Jambalaya 198

Rainbow Spring Rolls 201

Kale Quinoa & Apple Salad 202

Curry Cauliflower & Roasted Butternut Squash 205

Ultimate Vegetarian Lasagna 206

Sweet Potato Kale & Quinoa Cake 208

THE SWEET SPOT

Caramel & Fudge Snickers Brownie Cheese Cake 216

Red Velvet Cupcakes 219

Homemade Chocolate Chip Cookie & Ice-cream 220

Mini Sugar Cookie Fruit Tarts 223

Lemon Zest Sour Cream Donuts 224

Easy Chocolate Mousse Cake 227

Sweet Potato Cheesecake 228

Strawberry & Mascarpone Puffy Pastry 231

Salted Caramel Brownies 232

Deep Dish Apple Pie 235

Mini Blueberry & Lemon Bundt Cake 236

Irish Cream Crème Brulé 239

Angel Food Mixed Berry Short Cake................................. 240

Cinnamon Buns.. 243

IT'S 5'CLOCK SOMEWHERE

8 Most Popular Wines.. 247

Glassware & Tool Guide..251

The 6 Basic Spirits... 254

White Wine Sangria 261

Jalapeno Paloma... 262

CBD Blackberry Mule... 265

Cucumber Gimlet.. 266

Raspberry Lemonade Mimosa.. 269

Mint Julep.. 270

Spicy Bloody Mary.. 273

Red Wine Sangria... 274

Cadillac Margarita.. 277

Rosemary Old Fashion.. 278

Penicillin 281

The French Connection... 282

French 75... 285

Classic Dirty Martini... 286

ACKNOWLEDGEMENT

www.ingramcontent.com/pod-product-compliance
Lightning Source LLC
Chambersburg PA
CBHW080545230426
43663CB00015B/2710